Arthur Tappan Pierson

Seven years in Sierra Leone

The Story of the Work of William A. B. Johnson

Arthur Tappan Pierson

Seven years in Sierra Leone
The Story of the Work of William A. B. Johnson

ISBN/EAN: 9783744757195

Printed in Europe, USA, Canada, Australia, Japan

Cover: Foto ©Lupo / pixelio.de

More available books at **www.hansebooks.com**

Seven Years in Sierra Leone

THE STORY OF THE WORK OF

William A. B. Johnson

MISSIONARY OF THE CHURCH MISSION-
ARY SOCIETY FROM 1816 TO 1823 IN RE-
GENT'S TOWN, SIERRA LEONE, AFRICA

BY THE REV.

Arthur T. Pierson, D.D.

Author of "The Crisis of Missions," "The New Acts of the Apostles,"
"Many Infallible Proofs," etc., etc.

NEW YORK   CHICAGO   TORONTO

Fleming H. Revell Company

Publishers of Evangelical Literature

TO

MY DEARLY BELOVED FRIEND

THE REV. DONALD FRASER
OF LIVINGSTONIA, SOUTH AFRICA

WHO, WHILE THESE CHAPTERS WERE IN PREPARATION, WAS ON HIS WAY TO THE DARK CONTINENT; AND TO THE VAST BAND OF STUDENT VOLUNTEERS, WHOM HE REPRESENTS, AND WHO ARE LEADING ON THE MODERN CRUSADE OF MISSIONS FOR "THE EVANGELIZATION OF THE WORLD IN OUR GENERATION," THIS RECORD OF A PIONEER VOLUNTEER AND HIS GREAT WORK FOR GOD IS MOST LOVINGLY INSCRIBED

CONTENTS

CHAP.		PAGE
	PREFACE	7
I.	MADE MEET FOR THE MASTER'S USE	13
II.	THE LAND OF THE SHADOW OF DEATH	34
III.	RIGHTLY DIVIDING THE WORD OF TRUTH	54
IV.	SOUND OF ABUNDANCE OF RAIN	75
V.	FIRST-FRUITS UNTO GOD	94
VI.	FLOODS UPON THE DRY GROUND	114
VII.	THE REGIONS BEYOND	139
VIII.	IN THE FURNACE OF AFFLICTION	163
IX.	THE CLOUD OF WITNESSES	182
X.	AT THE DESIRED HAVEN	198
	APPENDICES	215

PREFACE

THERE is an old story of a reed-lute which, in its original rude, crude, native simplicity, gave forth notes of unusual sweetness. Some one, thinking to improve it, varnished and gilded it. It henceforth lost its peculiar power. It shone with the glitter of gold, but it no longer breathed the sweet purity of melody as before.

To preserve the simplicity of a little child, amid the maturity of manhood and the dignity of increasing responsibility and enlarging usefulness, is of foremost consequence, but it represents a gem as rare as it is radiant. It has been said that, while human development is from the cradle onward, the highest Christ-life is from the cross backward to the cradle: it is the man becoming a babe and, in a good sense, remaining a babe, never losing the childlike spirit; for it is the little ones that get the caresses, held closest to the bosom of the Father, cherished and nurtured in fondling arms.

Some twenty or more years ago I came across an anonymous memoir of William A. B. Johnson, now out of print. It was a stray copy, and in more than one sense it was a rare book. It impressed me then as, on the whole, the most remarkable story of seven years of missionary labor that I had ever read; and now, after a score of years of research into missionary history and biography, that judgment is unhesitatingly reaffirmed.

Such a narrative should not remain out of reach of those who delight in the study of missions. It is one of God's witnesses, and its voice ought not to be silent. Hence this humble effort to give Mr. Johnson's work and witness a wider hearing by reproducing the essential features of the narrative.

The original memoir appears to have been hastily prepared, and consists almost wholly of extracts from the missionary's diary. While there is, therefore, in it the continuity of time and chronological order, there is no logical arrangement of matter, no grouping of events in classes, and hence no effective contrasts such as show at a glance the wonderful results wrought by the gospel. The aim in this recasting of the narrative has been so to rearrange the matter contained in the memoir as to enable the reader to see as in a panorama the progress of the gospel triumphs in the most disheartening and desperate field which, eighty years ago, defied missionary conquest.

Much that the original journal of Johnson and the former memoir contained is here omitted, as either lacking relevancy or involving repetition. The story must speak for itself, but it would be incredible were not the facts too abundantly attested to allow of doubt. Nothing is more noticeable than the simple, humble, self-distrustful spirit which Mr. Johnson preserved to the end of his life. Perhaps this was the grand secret of his success. The lute never took on the fatal varnish and gilding of self-sufficiency and self-glory. He never ceased to be a little child; he waited to be led, to be taught, to be upheld, uplifted, upborne; even success never elated or inflated him; and the consequence was that God could be glorified in him as in few others, for he never himself got in the way of the cross. Always behind it, never before it, the crucified Christ was exalted, and proved His words that if He be lifted up He will draw all men unto Him.

As J. Hudson Taylor well says, while some are anxious to be "successors of the apostles," it may be well to seek to be successors of the Samaritan woman, who, while they went for food, but brought back no inquiring soul, forgot herself, her wants, and her water-pot, in her zeal to lead other sinners to her Saviour's feet.

The story of these seven years in Sierra Leone illustrates the great truth that to be grandly useful we need only to surrender ourselves wholly to God's hands. Like Mrs. Stowe in the writing of "Uncle Tom's Cabin," Johnson had no thought of doing any great thing. He did not wish to be famous. A door opened before him, and he entered it. A work was before him, and he undertook it for God, or rather he consented to have God do all the work, feeling himself to be only a tool, a vessel, in the Master's hand. And, as God always does when He finds a perfectly willing instrument, He wrought mightily through him, and compelled all who saw it to confess, "Surely this is the finger of God."

It has been well said of another book written on Africa that it supplies "a text for a scoffer." This narrative, on the contrary, furnishes a whole volume of apologetics and evidences for a true believer.

The author of this present volume has no higher desire than that the perusal of this pathetic and romantic story of a heroic life may prompt many to follow in the same path of consecrated service, and that it may prove a special encouragement and inspiration to the great body of Student Volunteers in the new missionary crusade.

ARTHUR T. PIERSON.

1127 DEAN STREET, BROOKLYN, N. Y., 1897.

SEVEN YEARS IN SIERRA LEONE

CHAPTER I

MADE MEET FOR THE MASTER'S USE

The preparation of the instrument is the first step in service. Aristotle says in effect that without some mixture of madness there is no great genius, and that nothing grand or superior is ever spoken, except by an agitated soul.

There is a truth akin to this in spiritual life. Stagnation is death. Without action and warmth there is no power. The genius of goodness, the energy of service, are always accompanied with the heart-heat of holy ardor, fervor, zeal, often with a fanaticism that cold critics stigmatize as madness; a passion for souls that keeps the whole being in a sublime agitation makes inaction more wearisome than the most exhausting labors. "We must not be afraid," said the lamented Keith Falconer, "of being ridiculed as eccentric. Eccentric is out of center, and he who is revolving about Christ and concentric—in center—as to Him, will be eccentric—out of center—as to the world."

Of these principles the subject of this sketch was a unique example and illustration. He was strangely moved by a mighty passion for Christ and for men—divinely agitated, for God's angel stirred the pool of his being; but the agitation was the sign of healing virtue in the waters, and the man so moved to his depths became a Bethesda to those who were sick and deformed and crippled by sin. Yet so manifest was it that in him God had chosen the poor, weak, despised nothing, in human eyes, to bring to naught the forms and forces of evil, that no one was either able or disposed to dispute that the excellency of the power was of God and not of men. This is a sufficient reason for giving prominence to this brief story of seven years: it furnishes so singularly luminous an example of the readiness of an omnipotent God to display His own strength and grace through an instrument manifestly too impotent to work such results in his own might.

It is now about eighty years ago when a young man from Hanover, Germany, applied to the Church Missionary Society for service in the mission field. He desired, with his wife, to engage in teaching. The application led to inquiry about them and an interview with them. Both applicants impressed the committee favorably; their personal character, views of truth, and singleness of aim commended them to the judgment of the society, and they were willing to give themselves entirely to the work of God. William Augustine Bernard Johnson was the name of the man, whose brief career is now to be outlined; and so satisfactory were the results of the committee's investigations that he and his wife were at once engaged to go as schoolmaster and schoolmistress to Africa, so soon as proper instruction had been given them.

Johnson was then working in a sugar-refinery in London, and the prompt acceptance of him on the part of the wise brethren of the committee proves that something in the man must have won for him golden opinions. It was certainly neither his looks nor his learning, for he was plain in person and comparatively uncultured. But there was a transparent guilelessness and earnestness of spirit which revealed itself from the first and which marked the applicant as no common man.

Some three years previous to this time he had been brought to the acceptance of Jesus as a Saviour by a somewhat remarkable dealing of God. He had been left to peculiar destitution, was ill clad and half starved. His wife was in bed, weak and weeping for hunger, and this doubled his distress. He cast himself on the bed and tossed in agony from side to side, feeling utterly friendless and forsaken, and not knowing how to get relief.

He had been taught, when a child of eight years, by his schoolmaster, to repeat on Monday mornings something of the sermon he had heard the day before; and a text which had thus long been fixed in memory now recurred to his mind:

> "Call upon Me in the day of trouble;
> I will deliver thee, and thou shalt glorify Me."

That promise had obtained its peculiar fastening in his mind in a somewhat curious way. When he repeated it to his schoolmaster he was rebuked because all he could recall was a *verse of Scripture*, and so that circumstance rooted it in his recollection. And now, after seventeen years, it came forcibly to his mind: "Call upon Me!" "Surely," he said, "this is a 'day of trouble.' Will He deliver me—me, who have sinned so against Him? And now may I, indeed, call upon God to deliver me?" As though the great white throne were set up and the "books were opened," he seemed to read the dark record of all his sins. He was in despair. No prospect here but want and woe, and no prospect beyond but a meeting with an angry God.

The next morning he went to work at the distillery, where he received the meager pittance of eighteen shillings sterling a week;

and, as he afterward confessed, he went with the feelings of a madman. When breakfast-hour came, and the other workmen left for home, he did the same, not expecting a meal, but only because to stay there would cause suspicion.

His wife met him at the door, smiling, and led him to an ample morning meal. Judge his astonishment to learn that a lady from India, who had taken a house near by, had applied to his wife for some one to stay with her, and had given her four shillings, bidding her put the house in order, and promising her further payments for her service.

The hungry man was amazed at the goodness of God, who had granted so merciful a deliverance, even in advance of being called upon; but his load of sin seemed only heavier, and he tried to pray, but seemed only to be adding sin to sin. In a vague hope of finding help in his despairing state, he went on the Friday following to a prayer-meeting held in the Savoy German church. There a Mr. Lehman, a Moravian missionary, gave an exhortation, telling of Jesus and His love for sinners, and how He came into the world to save them. Like young Spurgeon in the Primitive Methodist meeting-house in Colchester, —when the minister, preaching on the text, "Look unto Me, and be ye saved," seemed to be preaching right at him,—Johnson felt that the message was for him, and he cried to Jesus for mercy. He found he could pray, and believed that his sins were forgiven, and joy unspeakable and full of glory seemed to be pouring a new flood into his soul.

It was a marked conversion, and brought an assurance and confidence of his own saved state, that he was a child of God, which is essential for all true work for Christ. No man is fitted to guide a sinner to Christ who does not himself know the way, both doctrinally and experimentally. In all preaching the one commanding qualification—the very anointing of divine authority—is found in *experience.* We are witnesses, and witness is limited by personal knowledge. The deeper the hold on Christ, the mightier the grip on souls. Johnson had this basis of all qualifications: a clear, unmistakable conversion, an experience of grace; and was thus furnished with what Dr. Judson considered the great, first, indispensable requisite for a missionary, namely, a firm conviction and consciousness of his own conversion. He at once felt, like Dr. Duff, a great desire to be the means of conversion to his fellow-sinners, which he believed must be the case with every other true-hearted disciple. To him the experience of saving grace impelled and compelled a testimony. He began with his wife, whom he undertook to tell of his own renewal and to persuade to accept Christ; but he found that only God can bring a soul out of darkness into light. He then turned to his fellow-workmen, trying the same experiment, with the same result, being met by some of them with scornful laughter as though he were a fool, or by others with hateful sneers as though he were a hypocrite. His first efforts at faithful witnessing for Christ met only apathy, if not antipathy, yet even persecution did not drive him to silence.

The demand being made upon him for Sunday work, which he could not conscientiously meet, he left his situation for another, as warehouseman in a sugar-house in Prince's Place, Cable Street. He then joined the Savoy church, and was wont to go with his wife on Sunday evenings to Zion Chapel. By invitation of a young man, he went one Wednesday evening to Pell Street Chapel, where on the Sunday evening following he heard a Mr. Stodhardt preach, whom he was able to understand better than any other Christian minister whom he had hitherto heard. His text on that night was, "There is no peace, saith my God, to the wicked." He had never before heard so much of the Saviour of sinners, and was so attracted by this simple gospel message that henceforth he and his wife regularly attended at this place of worship. His half-informed mind staggered much at the doctrine of free and saving grace, but afterward, under the teachings of the Holy Spirit, these same truths became the staple of his whole ministry.

About the month of November, 1813, in a meeting at the chapel in Fetter Lane, where missionaries were addressed, Johnson was present; and there more than ever before he realized the high privilege and calling of a Christian disciple and the misery and wretchedness of the benighted heathen, and the yearning to tell them of Christ burst into a new flame. At first he felt that he himself could never go, having no real ability or education, and encumbered with an unconverted wife; but the constraint of love was upon him, and he offered himself to the Lord just as he was, saying, "Here am I; send me." That night he watered his couch with tears, turning his face to the wall and communing with the Lord out of the fullness of his heart.

No disciple ever takes his stand for God without finding Satan at his right hand to resist him, and it seemed as though the devil were heaping up damp rubbish and wet earth to quench the flame of holy desires. All sorts of discouragements and difficulties were piled up before him: he feared the society would not accept a married man, an ignorant man, a newly converted man. Such suggestions dragged him down into great darkness, and he even became careless and prayerless.

Again Mr. Stodhardt was used of God to

bring him relief. In a sermon he asked, "Are any of you in darkness? If so, search yourselves, for something is the reason why God hides His face." This remark compelled close examination, and Johnson saw that ever since he discouraged the desire for missionary work he had been sinking into deeper gloom. He was constrained to cry out, "Yes, that is it, that is it! With Thee nothing is impossible. Lord, send me! send me!" Thus the flame of missionary zeal was rekindled, and he was brought into closer relations with God, and every Christian grace seemed once more to flourish.

A new yearning for the conversion of his wife possessed him, that together they might join the church in Pell Street, which was close by his lodgings and had become such a Pool of Siloam in his spiritual blindness. Again Mr. Stodhardt's message proved a word from God. One of his remarks was that if we continue to pray for any particular blessing, in faith, it will surely be granted.* This stimulated more importunate and believing

* 1 John v. 15, 16.

intercession in his wife's behalf, and strengthened his confidence that a prayer-hearing God would single her out for a special blessing. Unbelief, always so persistent and subtle, for a time regained control, and again a horror of deep darkness seemed upon him. But the grace of God was so exceeding abundant that, while yet in this unbelieving state, his prayer for his wife was answered; for, while as a mere spectator she was looking on as the little band of disciples surrounded the table of the Lord at Pell Street Chapel, she was suddenly convinced of sin, of righteousness, and of judgment.

Her husband felt that he had now come into unclouded day. But so strangely successful are Satan's devices that, shortly after, another pall of gloom overspread him: his heart seemed as ice for coldness, and as stone or steel for hardness; he felt himself insensible to all divine impressions, and could not even pray.

Few human experiences are more remarkable as proofs of God's direct care over us than what may be called *gracious providences.*

At critical times such relief comes, from most unexpected sources, as demonstrates that He who alone knows our heart-sickness and faintness has sent us the exact medicine for our ills. For example, how often Mr. Stodhardt proved himself the messenger from above, the angel of the church, the channel of a divine communication to this benighted soul; in repeated instances, though himself unconscious of the fact, applying the balm of Gilead to the sore heart of Johnson! How was it—if we leave out God as the controlling and guiding power—that at this very time he was led to expound the first seven verses of Paul's first letter to Timothy, which are the only words specially addressed to such as "desire the office of a bishop"? And how was it that he was led to say that, when once a yearning is awakened in the heart for service in the ministry or any other particular calling, *if that yearning be enkindled by the Spirit of God*, it will prove a fire not easily quenched, and after every attempt to dampen or put it out will again burst into flame; in other words, a divinely created yearning cannot be silenced, but will not rest until it is accomplished. What wonder that a word so in season was an arrow in the heart of Johnson! He felt that so far as he had resisted this desire to be a missionary he had quenched the Spirit; and this conviction at first made the darkness deeper, until one day a promise of God brought again the day-dawn: "My grace is sufficient for thee: for My strength is made perfect in weakness."

He now sought Mr. Stodhardt and poured out his soul to him, and was advised by him to go to a Mr. A——, who often met with the committee of the London Missionary Society. He resolved to follow this counsel, and that night, also, fully to acquaint his wife with his strong desire after the mission field. Like Carey, he was met with a rebuff; she replied that she could not think of such a course for herself, preferring to stay where she was, but that if he wanted to go she would not keep him. Thus a new discouragement disheartened him; but he gave himself unto prayer, and so quickly did the answer come that but a few days later he found his wife moved by as great a desire as himself to go into the world field.

While waiting to hear the result of Mr. A——'s promised interposition with the committee of the London Missionary Society, he was told by Mr. Düring, who was in the employ of the Church Missionary Society, that they would send out with himself another laborer, and again hope was kindled that he might be chosen as Mr. Düring's companion. A conversation followed with Mr. Pratt, who brought the matter before the committee; and about a fortnight later both Mr. Johnson and his wife met the committee and were accepted, as has been recorded in the previous pages.

And now Johnson fell into a new snare. His wife became ill, and the temptation to despair because of his conscious inability and incompetency once more oppressed him; and yet again his pastor was the unconscious instrument of God in lifting him out of the horrible pit of despondency, by a sermon on these words: "Because the foolishness of God is wiser than men; and the weakness of God is stronger than men."* As though to emphasize the fitness of his message, Mr. Stodhardt, in connection with this discourse, chanced to mention a fellow-student, who after three years at college could not so much as learn English grammar, and who nevertheless was greatly used as a preacher of the good news.

Strange as it may seem, even with such support, Johnson sank down again into the miry clay of doubt, and so deeply that he began to question whether he was himself a saved man. Given over for a time to that fatal folly of morbid introspection, he kept searching into himself, as though anything but despondency could come from within, unless it were a confidence even more delusive. The great Adversary again tempted him to give up at once and forever all thoughts of mission work, and so to announce to the committee of the Church Missionary Society. But in a dream God spoke to him, and that precious promise which once before had proved a rock beneath his feet—"My grace

* 1 Cor. i. 25.

is sufficient for thee"—became to this lowly disciple what it had been to the great apostle to the Gentiles, a firm standing-place and resting-place. God so powerfully impressed on his mind His own all-sufficiency as to remove absolutely all his fear. Let not the reader fail to note how conspicuous was the intervention of God's inspired Word at every crisis of Johnson's experience. Whenever deliverance came, it came through the infallible Book, and so it was to the close of life. He never fell into any snare without finding relief and release in the Holy Scriptures both for himself and for others. How true it is: "The entrance of Thy words giveth light"!

A new doubt now arose, with regard to the place of his destination. There was in the entire world field no darker spot than Sierra Leone. Mary Lyon used to say to the girls at Holyoke, "If you would be true servants of God, be ready to go where no one else will;" and it was just such a test which was now applied to this humble believer. He was warned that the district of the Dark Continent for which he was designated represented the intensity of its darkness, the worst of its habitations of iniquity and cruelty. The final question, the supreme test, now to be applied to him was: Are you willing to go where no one else will?

Thus far in this volunteer's experience there had been little else than a series of disappointments, discouragements, and delays. Is there no lesson to be learned from God's strange way of dealing with this His chosen servant? Has it not been a common experience of those whom God calls to and fits for some special service, that at the very outset they are severely tested as to the sincerity of their self-surrender and the persistency of their purpose?

When Christ said to Simon Peter, "Whither I go, thou canst not follow Me now," he impetuously and impatiently replied, "Lord, *why* cannot I follow thee *now?* I am ready to go with Thee both to prison and to death. I will lay down my life for Thy sake." Jesus calmly answered: "Wilt thou lay down thy life for My sake? Verily, verily, I say unto thee, The cock shall not crow this night, till thou hast thrice denied that thou knowest Me."

Here was a disciple that loved Jesus, and felt both desirous to go anywhere with Him and ready to follow Him at risk of imprisonment and death. He was sincere, but he did not know himself; and even after this awful warning he was still so self-complacent and self-confident that he only the more vehemently declared his devotion to his Master at any cost. But the omniscient eye saw Satan at that moment preparing for his unwary feet a snare into which he would fall—saw that he would commit a sin of denial next in guilt to Judas's betrayal, and that his faith would utterly fail but for his Master's prayers.

The warning is plain. A sincere and earnest disciple, who feels ready to go at once, anywhere, at any risk, for his Lord's sake, may be impetuous in spirit and impatient of divine delays. Perhaps the Lord sees that he does not know himself, that he needs the test of patient waiting. It may be, only a lapse into sin can show him how weak and wilful and wayward he is; that he must, in a sense, be "converted" before he can be used to strengthen his brethren; that perhaps he is not yet filled with the Spirit and must tarry until he is endued with power from on high.

There is singular pathos in those words, "Whither I go,"—to Gethsemane's passion and Golgotha's cross,—"thou canst not follow Me now; but thou shalt follow Me afterward." Not *now*. God's time may not yet be fully come, but our time is always ready. Yet is it not true that *we are least ready when we think we are most ready?* Resolute, indeed, but often in the crises of temptation resolution snaps like the green withes or new ropes which bound Samson; vehement, indeed, but much vehemence is the mere movement of fleshly energy, not the momentum of spiritual force and power. Carlyle quaintly says: "Vehemence is not strength. A man is not strong who takes convulsion-fits, though six men cannot hold him then."

The subsequent career of this missionary shows that he needed just this discipline of delay. He who would follow Christ must wait His beck and bidding, His time and way, and wait also for his own full testing and training. When we confidently feel ready for heroic martyrdom, He may see us on the verge of cowardly denial or betrayal. At every stage of service we must leave ourselves wholly in His hands. Even the chosen vessel needs cleansing and filling—it may be, needs breaking and remaking—before it will be "a vessel unto honor, sanctified, and meet for the Master's use, and prepared unto every good work."

CHAPTER II

THE LAND OF THE SHADOW OF DEATH

THAT must have been a weirdly awful scene when, in May, 1890, Henry Varley, the evangelist, preached to a throng of five thousand people in the vast crater of Mount Eden, New Zealand.

Johnson's appointed field of labor was a crater; not a burnt-out crater, but the very mouth of a burning, seething, restless hell of iniquity. As this small section of western Africa must so prominently figure in this biographical sketch, it is well to rehearse the peculiar circumstances under which Sierra Leone was settled.

Its name is due to the fancied resemblance of the contour of its hills to a lion's form. In 1787 a settlement was projected by Granville Sharp and other philanthropists, in order to provide a suitable home for destitute negroes from different parts of the world, as well as to establish a center whence a Christian civilization might reach out into other parts of the Dark Continent. At this time there were in London a large number of blacks whom it was desired to remove from the city for the relief of the city itself, and it was thought that Sierra Leone would afford a good colonial settlement for the several purposes in view. Four hundred and seventy destitute negroes were removed thereto in 1787 by the London committee. Eleven hundred and ninety-six others were sent there from Nova Scotia in 1790, the northern climate proving too severe for them. The population was further increased by other transportations of people of color, and, after the abolition of the slave-trade, in 1807, slaves captured by the British cruisers were put ashore there and settled. In 1789 the settlement had been plundered and destroyed by a band of pirates. Sharp, Wilberforce, and others had then formed the Sierra Leone Company, and Freetown became the center of the colony. The inhabitants suffered greatly from fever, and the French in 1794 made Sierra Leone the scene of further inroads and plunders. After the reëstablishment of the colony it was finally transferred, in 1808, to the British government, since which time it has steadily advanced.

This was the field of labor to which William Johnson was to go, and it is not strange if, as he thought of the scene of his labors, it presented little attraction. He could not forget that there was the dumping-ground for the world's refuse population, ignorant and degraded people, rescued from the holds of slave-ships, or exported from overcrowded cities like London, where they had become an intolerable stench in the nostrils of the community. As Johnson thought of such a hopeless field of work, a darkness that might be felt seemed to envelop him. But once again there came to him light through a promise of God.

> "I will bring the blind by a way that they knew not;
> I will lead them in paths they have not known:
> I will make darkness light before them,
> And crooked things straight.
> These things will I do unto them, and not forsake them." *

* Isaiah xlii. 16.

On the eleventh day of March, 1816, Johnson and his wife embarked on board the *Echo*, sailing for Sierra Leone, and the missionary career of this devoted servant of God was thus actually begun. On the 27th of April following, with Messrs. Horton, Düring, Jost, and their wives, they reached Freetown in safety. The voyage had not been without incidents of interest. Twice divine deliverances had been wrought in answer to prayer —once when Johnson was taken dangerously ill, and again when by some carelessness or mismanagement the ship had been driven so close to the rocks that it was almost impossible to avoid its being dashed in pieces.

When the missionaries, meeting at Sierra Leone, divided up the field among the laborers, Hogbrook, afterward known as Regent's Town, was appointed as Johnson's particular station. He was candidly made acquainted with the fact that many negroes were there, and in a fearful slough of mingled wickedness, woe, and want. But—keeping that promise before him, "I will bring the blind by a way that they knew not," and feeling that he had not chosen the field for himself, but had been chosen by God for the field—instead of being driven into darkness by the unpromising aspects of his work, he found light in looking up to God and was enabled even to rejoice and exult in Him. A deep conviction possessed him, at the outset, that God's Spirit both could and would uphold him and his fellow-laborers in their humble efforts, and make them the means of salvation to multitudes of these debased negroes. In this strong faith we may find a prophecy of the actual results. "We are saved by hope." Despair never yet achieved anything but disaster. There was something about Johnson that led others to expect results. Mr. Bickersteth, who had arrived about six months earlier, soon discerned the worth of a man of such consecrated spirit, so dead to the world and self, and so devoted to the Lord; and he early predicted that, wherever the providence of God might place Johnson, a blessing would surely follow.

Among Johnson's earliest utterances in his new field was a memorable tribute to the power of God's Spirit, which is here put prominently in the forefront of the narrative, since it is of main consequence, not so much that we trace even so remarkable a career, as that we penetrate to those secrets of success which are, like God Himself, essentially the same yesterday and to-day and forever.

Among the earliest entries in his journal, he records how, when confronted with the terrible degradation and depravity of the Hogbrook negroes, he felt "fully convinced that if God the Holy Spirit stopped them, as it were, in their mad career, although some of the wildest cannibals in Africa, they could not any longer resist." This is another factor in this marvelous career which explains its manifold and multiplied successes. Two we have already noticed—the constant resort for guidance to the infallible Book of God, and the bold approach in prayer to the throne of grace. Here is the third: William Johnson honored and trusted the Holy Spirit of God. Keeping these three great facts full in view, we shall need no other philosophy to account for these seven years in Sierra Leone.

Soon after Johnson's arrival at the colony he went to the Yongroo district to introduce Bell's system of education. Its author, Andrew Bell, D.D.—who was born at St. Andrews in 1753, and died in 1832—while at Madras acting as chaplain, was intrusted by the directors of the East India Company with the management of the school for the education of the orphans of the European militia. He obtained the services of well-qualified teachers, and adopted the expedient of conducting the school by the aid of the pupils themselves. Hence originated the famous "monitorial system," so called, whereby the school or family might teach itself under the superintendence of a master or parent. This method is here briefly outlined because Johnson availed himself of it in the educational work of the colony.

He found the children more active and quick to apprehend than he had expected. While in the Yongroo district he also met two natives, each of whom came to him saying, "Me wish to learn Book; me know nothing;" and whom he began at once to teach to read the Word of God, this experience being a forecast and foretaste of what he was afterward to see more largely developed—the intense desire for a knowledge of the divine Book.

In June, less than two months after landing, Johnson removed to Hogbrook, where he found fifteen hundred released slaves waiting to be taught. As he looked upon this mixed company—the very refuse of humanity—he felt that no mere human teaching could reach and raise them to any higher dignity; but he planted his faith firmly on this conviction: that with God nothing is impossible, and that it was *the lost* that Jesus came to seek and to save. He remembered that God's Word is a hammer that breaks in pieces the flinty rock, and that God's Spirit is a fire that melts and subdues all things; and he undertook his work, simply waiting on God, confidently trusting in almighty power and love, dependently looking to the Holy Spirit to give all increase, and willing and desirous that all praise, honor, and glory should accrue to God alone. Every word above written should be weighed and pondered. We are starting out on a path of narration in which are to be traced some of the most marvelous signs of God's working since apostolic days; and it is first of all needful, for the full profit of this study, that we fix in our minds the human conditions which made it possible for divine power to be so singularly exhibited.

Let repetition first make emphatic the absolute hopelessness of this field of labor to human eyes. Johnson's first impressions no subsequent changes could ever efface. He could never forget the scene engraved on his mind and heart as he first looked on the degraded herds of human swine at Hogbrook. As Livingstone confessed a half-century later in the wilds of equatorial Africa, he felt as though he were in hell itself and breathing the sulphurous atmosphere of the bottomless abyss. Such utter wretchedness and unspeakable vileness he had never before seen; and, withal, sin brought forth death literally, for six or seven died in a day.

Again he said within himself, "Is there any hope?" But he dared not give way to despair.

Could not God make visible even to these and among these, who were the offscouring of the world, His saving power? The words of Jesus came with strange force to his mind: "So the last shall be first, and the first last." And so he freshly resolved, "I will simply go and tell these poor creatures of the love of Christ, and rest on God's promise, 'My word shall not return unto Me void.'"

He began at once to carry out his purpose. He found very few of them who could speak even a broken English. The greater proportion of them, being taken from slave-ships and originally captured from different African tribes, were, of course, ignorant of one another's language and had no common vehicle of conversation or communication, except a sort of dialect, generally found in such cases, in which English words were thrown together without grammatical forms or connections, but sufficiently intelligible to convey meaning. Of course the capacity to understand English was correspondingly limited, and their teacher found himself compelled to use only such words and sentences as are of the simplest sort, adapted to a child's mind and measure of intelligence.

It was a happy circumstance that it was not necessary to describe what he found in this new field. The misery of Hogbrook, or Regent's Town, could not be conceived by an outsider even if adequately portrayed, but it could not be put in words. He found some in an actual state of starvation, and to them it was his business to deal out rations of food first of all. He was himself living in a leaky hut, with no bed but the ground, with no covering but a blanket, his wife remaining elsewhere until a decent dwelling could be built at Hogbrook. He describes himself as "in a wilderness," but adds: "'In the wilderness shall waters break out, and streams in the desert. And the parched ground shall become a pool, and the thirsty land springs of water.'" Thus did the Lord prove to His servant the truth of His own promise that, when God's words are found and we do eat them, they are the joy and rejoicing of our hearts. There is some message of God supplied for every time of need.

Another discouragement threatened the work just begun: the strongest member of this little missionary band was the first to succumb to the treacherous African climate, namely, Mr. Jost; but God sustained Johnson. He strengthened himself in the Lord and with new vigor took up daily duty as one who has been forcibly reminded that the time is short.

The influence of superstition is enslaving in proportion to the otherwise low level of the poor victims who are in bondage to it. Ignorance is the mother of superstition, and, because the ignorance of these natives was extreme, their fears were correspondingly easy to excite and hard to allay. The worship of fetishes is inseparable from such a low level, and in his whole experience among these people Johnson found the power of gree-grees immense. These are charms, whose fascination consists, more than anything else, in the mystery which invests them. A piece of buffalo hide or alligator's skin, within which is sewed up an unknown something,—a bit of an elephant's tooth, a serpent's fang or rattle, a strip of parchment with a few characters from the Koran, a piece of glass, or almost anything else, with or without value,—suffices to command a veneration scarcely second in degree to the homage paid to the most august and gigantic idol. On one of his mission tours in the colony Johnson found a very superstitious man, who had formerly lived at Regent's Town, but had left it for some district less enlightened by the gospel, where he could live more securely after the fashion of his pagan countrymen. In a word, he was one who, doing evil, hates the light and withdraws into the darkness to escape its reproving ray. He was in bondage to gree-grees; and in hope to show him the worthlessness of his charms—the powerlessness of his little god—Johnson had cut open the leather in which one was sewed and found it to contain nothing but a piece of paper—the old wrapper belonging to a cake of soap, and upon which was the stamp of the manufacturer, "Genuine Windsor Soap." The vain charm was exposed to the man and his companions, evoking hearty laughter. This gree-gree had a history that is instructive and suggestive. Its owner had bought it, for one shilling and threepence sterling, of a Mandingo man, a Mohammedan—an example of the way in which these deluded people are practised upon by Moslems. And yet these greegrees and "devils' houses" were then to be seen everywhere through the colony.

One of the deepest shadows which the missionary found, even in this land of the death-shade, was the complete degradation of the people, and the utter inadequacy of such terms as they understood to convey any proper conceptions of divine things. This double discouragement confronted him everywhere, and would have confounded him, had he not remembered that the things which are impossible with men are possible with God. Here were minds and hearts so brutalized with sin and so fossilized into insensibility that to make any wholesome impression on them seemed hopeless; and the only medium of conveying such impression was language that had sunk to their own low level. He who is to lift men needs a lifting force, and in this case the force, or at least the fulcrum, was what was lacking.

For example, William Davis went toward Cockle Bay to speak to his country-people of Jesus, and, on returning, told Johnson that he met some natives, whom he besought to go to Wilberforce to hear Mr. Gates preach, but who replied that, as they did not understand English, they could not even pray to God. There was in this a deeper meaning than they knew, for their vernacular was so hopelessly interwoven with their abominations and superstitions that it seemed incapable of conveying Christian ideas. Mr. Davis had indeed assured them that He who knows our desires and thoughts can read the heart's longing even through the most imperfect dialect, but we must not lose sight of the fact that such native speech presented a mountain obstacle in the way of gospel triumph.

Again, the shadow of imported vices rested on this land. It was found necessary to explain to these slaves the word "Christmas" and the meaning of the festivities associated with our Lord's nativity. There had been introduced, by Europeans, a custom of almost universal intoxication; every one made as much noise as possible, and gunning, dancing, drumming, and most other forms of boisterous and riotous celebration disgraced the sacred day, carried to a great pitch of revelry. But now Johnson had the joy of noting that not a single person was intoxicated, nor was there any unusual noise or disturbance on Christmas day. A reverent audience met at the service of worship in the morning, and in the evening he went to Leicester Mountain to hold a missionary prayer-meeting, accompanied by a crowd of about four hundred men, women, and children.

The slave-trade added to all other curses which rested upon Africa a darkness which might be felt. It filled him with an unspeakable horror, which reminds one of Livingstone's chronic impression about what he called the "open sore of the world." As cargo after cargo was landed from rescue ships, and human beings were left to be cared for, and in the most deplorable condition, from two hundred to as many as from eight hundred to twelve hundred at one time, Johnson felt as though a door had been opened into hell itself, giving him some faint conception of the miseries of lost souls. These rescued slaves were in every way living pictures and parables of woe and want, wretchedness and wickedness. The women especially were sufferers; most of all, the girls from ten to twelve years of age. Most of the children were taken ill, and many of them died, too weak to resist disease. And, but for the unselfish love that bore him up as in everlasting arms, he acknowledged that he would rather have been shut up in a dungeon than have been compelled to behold the sufferings, hear the sighs and groans, and witness the dying agonies of these victims of man's inhumanity to man. To save their lives seemed a vain hope, and in some respects scarcely desirable, for it meant a prolongation of misery. To save their souls seemed even more impossible in the brief time and amid the limited opportunities which were available.

To add to the afflictions of this humble servant of God, ophthalmia, which had broken out at Regent's Town, had seized upon his eyes, so that he could scarcely see.

And yet, amid all these surroundings, this man of God undertook to hold forth that Word which is at once light and life. The church and school-house stood together on one hill, in a large inclosure. The remainder of the hill contained about twelve acres, and, with the help of the children, was early brought into a state of cultivation, which promised in another year to furnish nearly if not quite enough provision for the school tables. At the close of the year 1817, and after a residence of only eighteen months, William Johnson could rejoicingly contemplate an improvement so rapid, regular, and far-reaching that it may be questioned whether the like of it has been seen elsewhere in missionary history. We have searched the annals of the century without finding any parallel, unless perhaps it be found in such astonishing victories of the gospel as have been exhibited in the Hawaiian Islands, in the Telugu Mission in India, in Banza Manteke in equatorial Africa, and in northern Formosa under George L. MacKay. Yet in some respects what Johnson saw in Sierra Leone surpasses, as it also precedes, them all.

This godly missionary found himself at the close of this year, without any assistance, amid labors, both temporal and spiritual, which were overwhelming. The people to whom he ministered were like feeble bulbs set in the soil, with scarce life enough to survive, and needing constant watching and nursing in order to their growth or even continued existence. And he was so pressed and oppressed by the care of temporalities that he could not attend as he would to the higher interests of their souls. He had to oversee blacksmiths, masons, carpenters, attend to storekeeping and land-tilling, be a surveyor and a purveyor, teach and preach, feed bodies and feed souls, all at once. And yet he saw Hogbrook already, after eighteen months, becoming a garden of the Lord, where the spiritual features corresponded to the improving material aspect and attraction. The low brook which, running through the town, gave it its somhewat offensive name, was a symbol of the river of the water of life, which makes everything to live whither it cometh. In this unfruitful soil he sowed the double seed of the kingdom: first the Word of God, and secondly himself, content to fall into the ground and die that he might bring forth much fruit. And so it came to pass that, in this region and shadow of death, again it became true that "light is sprung up."

CHAPTER III

RIGHTLY DIVIDING THE WORD OF TRUTH

When Mrs. Ingalls in Burma found herself face to face with hundreds of thousands of unsaved souls, she could not withhold from them the message of salvation, and in her simple way, like the woman of Samaria, became the herald of the Saviour she had found. When by conservative ecclesiastics she was called to account for her itinerating tours, and asked, "Were you ever ordained to preach?" she replied, "No; but I was *forcordained.*"

William Johnson had originally been sent to Sierra Leone to teach school, but he had been thrust by the very exigencies of the field into the work of an evangelist, and had made full proof of his ministry. Though not commissioned nor ordained by man to preach, yet, in the presence of such want and woe, such spiritual destitution and spiritual inquiry, he could only say to himself, "I have no ability nor authority, but what can I do? My heart is full, and if I should hold my peace, the very stones would immediately cry out." It had always been his desire to preach the unsearchable riches of Christ, but he had felt his unworthiness so deeply that he doubted his call to this work. God Himself had now solved his perplexity in a very practical way by constraining him to become His witness in the presence of such abounding need and in the absence of any who were better qualified. The divine seal was on the work and on the workman, and it was plain that the Holy Spirit meant him for a service much more extended and important than was included in the first plan. He had unconsciously grown into a first-class missionary, and the committee in London felt that he should be formally invested with all proper authority for his wider work. Accordingly, letters were written calling a meeting of the missionaries, Butscher, Wylander, and Wenzel, for his ordination as a Lutheran minister.

Meanwhile nine more adults were baptized and other candidates were waiting. The Saturday evening prayer service was notably a time of special blessing, and that particular hour was marvelously owned of God. For example, on the first Saturday evening of January, 1817, while prayer was being offered to God, two young men cried out, "Jesus, Massa, have mercy," and with such demonstrations of deep feeling that the incident naturally prevented the orderly conduct of a prayer-meeting, as it distracted the attention of the people. The meeting was about closing when Johnson, going outside, found in a house near at hand a throng of negroes, some on their knees crying aloud, others sitting, but trembling and in tears, while yet others in their broken dialect were singing praises unto Jesus. Unable to pass by such a gathering, he went in and spoke to them of the new birth from above, in terms adapted to their simplicity. They heard him with much docility, but, when he proposed the singing of a hymn, their sobs choked their utterance, and when he attempted to pray, his voice was almost drowned by their loud outcries for mercy.

He recorded the fact that never before had he anywhere witnessed such a scene, and that waves of feeling swept over him like ocean tides as he beheld the workings of God on these hearts and consciences. Mingled astonishment and gratitude swayed him. He had come out to Sierra Leone asking of God one soul as his reward, and already beheld the abundant fruits of his labors apparent. At the six o'clock prayer-meeting of the Sunday morning these singular manifestations of God's mighty power were renewed, as also at the regular morning service, when he spoke from John xxi. 19: "Follow thou Me."

Experiences like these were, even at this early stage of his work, already so common that the entries in his journals are little more than a monotonous repetition or reiteration of the description of such scenes and incidents, so that examples need not be multiplied. It will suffice to add that such evidences that the Holy Spirit was directly dealing with the conscience and will were abundant throughout the whole period of Johnson's labors.

On the second Sunday of February, after the baptism of ten adults, the Lord's Supper was celebrated with forty-one communicants; and, as usual, Johnson dwelt upon the great themes of human guilt and divine grace. Without remembering his constant recurrence to these two foundation truths we shall miss the most important lesson of his ministry and the vital secret of his serviceableness. It may be well, therefore, to tarry just here and consider the bearing of the truth preached upon the whole power of our ministry to souls.

There is no accident in the moral universe. A law of cause and effect works in the realm of mind as in the realm of matter. God is not mocked by atheistic chance, with its hopeless uncertainties: every seed has its own body, and every sowing its own reaping, and the harvest is according to the tilling. Our own persuasion grows, as our observation and experience broaden our induction, that, as the Archbishop of Canterbury phrases it, it is the great primary truths of the gospel that most surely mold character. John the Baptist, last of the old seers, first of the new evangelists, was a voice proclaiming three great primitive truths: first, sin and judgment; second, the coming of One greater than he, to atone for sin and remove judgment; third, the present opportunity of faith in Him, whereby sin is effectually taken away before judgment lifts its awful ax of destruction. "Behold, the Lamb of God, who beareth away the sin of the world!" Here is one sentence, with its few, simple, primary teachings; and upon those foundations all practical theology may be constructed—the whole divine system of saving truth. Germs of doctrine, they are capable of endless expansion, but they nevertheless contain in themselves, germinally, all that we need to know in order to salvation.

It is a singular proof of the wisdom and grace of God that He has made the primary truths of salvation so few and so simple. He loved the world and yearned over the race. Salvation could be applicable to the whole family of man only as it was adapted to the lowest and least. There are vast multitudes, so sunk in sin and so small in intellectual capacity, that they can take in only the simplest primitive truths; and all of us, even the highest and greatest and wisest, have at last to return to and lean upon these same primitive truths.

The famous Bishop Butler, who has been called the Melchizedek of the Anglican Church, because he had neither predecessor nor successor, had days of darkness as he approached his dying hour. "What shall I lay hold of?" said he to his chaplain. He reminded the dying bishop of the atonement for sin. "But how shall I know that it is for *me*?" "'Him that cometh unto Me I will in no wise cast out,'" was the scriptural answer. "Oh, this is comfortable indeed!" said the bishop, as he rested, like any other poor sinner, upon the all-sufficiency of grace and the all-inclusiveness of the promise of God.

The late Bishop of Durham, one of the

greatest scholars and thinkers of his age, had, as he neared life's boundary, many weeks of quiet debility, favorable to meditative habits. His friends thought that his mighty mind might be brooding over some great problems of philosophy or theology. But he assured them it was not so. He said, "I take three or four great primitive truths and think upon them constantly." From all his excursions into the limitless realms of speculative thought he at last returned with the spirit of a little child to quench his thirst at the fountain of living waters, and, like Israel in the desert, drink of that Rock which is Christ.

Michael Faraday had the brains of twenty common men; yet when he was asked, as the last hours drew near, " What are your speculations?" calmly said, "Speculations? I have none. I am not resting my dying head on speculations. 'I know whom I have believed, and am persuaded that He is able to keep that which I have committed unto Him against that day.'"* And so, when Sir George Williams visited the dying Earl of

* 2 Tim. i. 12.

Shaftesbury, and found him, with face turned to the wall, in deep depression, he bent over and whispered in his ear, "'Complete in Him'—complete, that is, lacking nothing!" The departing earl turned over in bed and said, "Yes; that is just the message that I need now."

It is a well-known and very beautiful fact that both John Wesley and Charles H. Spurgeon, who in the next century in so many things closely resembled him, had similar experiences in approaching death. Wesley had several days of struggle with Satan, and deep darkness, and on coming out of the conflict he said:

"I the chief of sinners am,
But Jesus died for me!"

And Spurgeon, as he approached death, said to his friend Taylor of Norwood, "There are four words upon which I have lived and shall die." "What are they?" said Taylor. "They are these four," said Spurgeon: "*Jesus died for me!*"

We would affirm, what from time to time we shall emphasize by repetition in the course of this narrative, that we believe that the almost unprecedented triumph of William Johnson at Sierra Leone was owing mainly to three things: he heartily honored the Holy Spirit of God; he constantly communed with God in prayer; and he preached uniformly the great primary truths of the gospel. What we just now desire to make emphatic is that he did not neglect those severer aspects of truth which are necessary if we are to arouse sinners to a sense of danger and make them appreciate their need of Christ. For instance, one Sunday morning he took as his theme the day of judgment, with the state of the saints in heaven and of the wicked in hell. One hearer, William Tamba, went home much alarmed, tried to pray, but could not, tried to sleep, but could not, and when at length he wearily fell into slumber, he had a dreadful dream. He saw a man coming into his cottage and making in the middle of it a large fire; then bringing in two persons, he bound them with chains and put them into the fire. Tamba in his dream beheld the nails dropping from their fingers and toes, and he saw that they were not dead, but howling with anguish. At length the man came to Tamba himself and prepared to thrust him also into the fire, when another voice from behind solemnly said, "Let him alone; he belongs to Me!" Whereupon he was set at liberty at once. So vivid was this dream that when he fully awoke he found himself upon his knees before his bed. He continued in tears and prayers all night, and early the next day came to Johnson, asking, like the Philippian jailer, "What must I do to be saved?" and when an explanation of his inquiries was sought, he related his dream of the night preceding.

How far Johnson was from any mere pride of numbers may be seen from the fact that in his letter to the secretaries in October, 1821, he said: "I cannot say how many communicants we have. The number is great; I am afraid to number them."

In 1822 he again wrote to the secretaries, specifying where missionaries or schoolmasters were needful, and he added, "Missionaries who will simply preach Christ crucified will alone succeed." He said: "None of the

Gentiles have been more injured than Africa, and no people is more degraded. It is time to assume the character of the widow who pleaded, 'Avenge me of mine adversary.' I plead not mine own case, but the widowhood of Africa; for her will I cry with importunity, 'Send missionaries! send missionaries! Avenge Africa of her adversary!'"

The school work formed a conspicuous feature in the labors of Johnson at Hogbrook. When the bell first rang for school, ninety boys, besides all the girl-pupils, made their appearance, and he formed them into four classes. At six o'clock in the evening another school was opened for adults, with twelve women and thirty-one men. In this as in all other forms of service the sole dependence was on the Word of God, and the unceasing prayer was for the Holy Spirit to reveal the truth and power of God to the soul. Few of Christ's servants ever presented a parallel to the simple, humble, single-minded faith and devotion of this missionary, and few triumphs of the gospel present a parallel to the story of these seven years at Sierra Leone. Do not these two facts bear the relation of cause and effect? Is success such as we now begin to chronicle an accident or a mere incident, or is it simply a natural harvest of the unmixed seed of the kingdom, steeped in tears and sown in faith?

The school grew so fast that there was no room; fifty boys were crowded on the piazza and others under the shade of trees. Meanwhile the church building was in erection, where, as soon as ready, it was proposed to hold both school and services of worship. So pressing were the spiritual needs of this people that it was deeply regretted that any time must be given to secular cares and affairs; but in all matters he sought to act as a partner with God. He yearned also to go into neighboring villages and teach the Word of God, where the English tongue was better or more widely understood; but for the time he was compelled to give all heed to the destitution immediately about him, wishing he could multiply himself a hundredfold.

Every work finds unbelieving hinderers. When the schools and congregations were outgrowing all accommodations—and such hunger was manifested to hear the Word of God that the people pressed upon him as upon his Master, so that there was no room even about the door—there were those who stood off and shook their heads ominously; and who discouraged him, saying that Africans are all like a tornado, which comes all at once and with a rush, but soon blows over. But his trust was too strongly fixed in God to be easily turned aside. He was confident that such a desire to hear and read the Word of God could come only from the Spirit of God, and had therefore upon it the seal of continuance. Meanwhile, despite all the predictions of doubters and unbelievers, the day-school increased to a hundred and forty boys and women, and grew in interest as well as numbers. A stone church capable of holding some five hundred was roofed in, in August, and a fourth Sunday had not passed after its opening before the building was already too small for the people.

Thus, in a few months after landing, we have found Johnson settled in the spot where the rest of his short life was to be spent, and where, by God's blessing, a desert of sin and Satan was rapidly to change into a garden of the Lord. His labors were so great that from one Sunday to another he could scarce find a single hour for himself. Captured negroes continued to arrive from time to time, and sometimes as many as a thousand at once. He was obliged to send for rice every week to Freetown, five miles off, and distribute these rations twice a week without assistance. At times it seemed as though one man could not bear up under such burdens, and he was on the point of giving up in despair. But the thought that he might be the means which God would use to bring even this benighted people to the feet of Jesus, nerved and fortified him for undertakings so laborious and various that they remind us of the toils and trials of Paul.

The gospel proved itself again the true civilizer. Idleness and ignorance are the handmaids of vice and impiety, as industry and intelligence are the handmaids of virtue and godliness. Surprising as it may seem, this debased people already began to show improvement in the matter of cleanliness and thrift. These filthy slaves studied personal tidiness, and strove to get properly attired to appear before the Lord on Sunday. The Rev. Joel Lindley, of the Zulu Mission, used to say that the first sign of new life in the natives was a desire to be clad. A man would come to the mission premises to barter something for a cheap calico shirt, then a few days after for a pair of duck pants, and then for a little three-legged stool; and, said Dr. Lindley, "when that Zulu got on his shirt and pants and sat down on his little stool he was about a mile above the level of the naked savages about him." And so, often the earliest indication that the poor negroes of Hogbrook were aspiring to a new life was a desire to appear washed and cleanly clad.

As Johnson continued speaking twice a day and thrice on Sundays, the people thronged him as though to ask further knowledge concerning the ways of God. At times he found them seeking clothing or other supplies for temporal needs, and he began to suspect that they were moved by no higher motive than selfish desire of gain. But this was only a symptom of general improvement, as abundant facts attested.

In October of that first year a shingle-maker, by name Joe Thompson, following him from church, asked to speak with him. With a holy gratitude he found that this man was a religious inquirer, seeking relief, not for his body, but for his soul, under a load of conscious sin and guilt; and he proved *the first convert unto Christ at Sierra Leone.*

It was natural that the missionary should take special interest in this, the first-fruits of his work; and, seeking to trace the means used of God for his awakening, he found that one evening, when he had asked his hearers if any of them had ever given five minutes to prayer to Jesus, this young mechanic had been so struck with the question, which he could answer only to his own condemnation, that it proved an arrow of God, wounding him and working deep conviction of sin. He had afterward heard some explanation of what misery sin entails, and what is the present and future state of the unforgiven sinner. Something within witnessed that the Word of God was true. All the evil deeds and thoughts of his life moved as in awful procession before his mind and memory. He had tried to pray, but could not, and it was at this stage that he sought his pastor to learn from him what he must do to be saved.

Imagine the sensations which thrilled that humble missionary, when God gave him, out of that offscouring of the world, the first precious jewel for his crown! Let him give his own testimony: "What at that moment I felt is unspeakable. I pointed this inquirer to the crucified Jesus, and the tears ran down his cheeks. I was obliged to leave him, for I could not contain myself. I went home and fell on my knees."

First drops betoken a shower. The next week more inquirers came in like manner, and the doubts and fears of Johnson as to his mission were at once banished. There was no more room to question that God had sent him thither, for He was daily with him.

Soon after, at his request, Mr. Butscher, stationed at Leicester Mountain, came over and baptized twenty-two of these captured slaves, among whom was one boy. As they were individually and carefully examined as to their knowledge of Christ, before this ordinance was administered, both Mr. Johnson and Mr. Butscher were astonished to see in what manifest and manifold ways God had revealed Himself to these ignorant sons of Ham. Within nine months after Johnson's arrival over forty had received baptism.

How simple were the sermons which were so used of God may appear from a few specimens which will be found in this short sketch. For example, a discourse on 1 Corinthians ii. 2: "1. Who is Jesus Christ? 2. What has Jesus Christ done? 3. What is Jesus Christ doing to-day? 4. What is Jesus Christ going to do?" This would hardly be accepted as a model in homiletics or hermeneutics, but it was made the means of salvation, which is the highest proof of efficiency in a sermon; for, if none were found to praise the archer and his bow, there were groans from the wounded which proved that the rude arrow had somehow hit the mark.

Prayer and testimony meetings became a natural necessity, for those whom God had awakened yearned over others, and desired to tell one another what God had done for their souls. Affecting confessions were made from time to time in these prayer-meetings. For example, Johnson preached on Sunday, May 13, 1821, on Isaiah xliv. 21. The sermon made an impression so profound that the next evening a man came to him and made a remarkable disclosure of his own state, and showed that the Word of God had been to him a mirror in which he was surprised to see himself and his people so wonderfully reflected that he could only exclaim, "God knows all things; He put them things in the Bible." He saw that no human being could have so portrayed the condition of a people he had never seen.* Thus by manifold signs wrought through this simple

* Appendix I.

preacher and teacher, who declared the whole counsel of God, who preached the law and the gospel, rightly dividing the Word of truth, God set His seal on this His servant, and enabled him to make full proof of his ministry.

CHAPTER IV

SOUND OF ABUNDANCE OF RAIN

THERE is in mechanics, as in nature, a *law of adjustment*, upon which all harmonious and successful action and interaction depend. Until one part meets its fellow-part in exact articulated adaptation the organism cannot have healthy activity. Until every wheel, lever, cog, and even screw, is in its place no machine, if there be motion at all, can move without friction.

Some such thought as this is suggested in that divinely inspired prayer which sums up the Epistle to the Hebrews: "The God of peace . . . make you perfect in every good work to do His will, working in you that which is well pleasing in His sight."* The leading word (καταρτισαι) means, adjust you thor-

* Heb. xiii. 20, 21.

oughly, knit or frame you together, articulate you as a joint in the body to the framework of the body. Only so can God work in you to will and to do. And it is equally plain that so soon as we are thus adjusted to the work and will of God blessing will follow, for God is free to work.

Doubtless no further explanation is needed to account for the immediate success of Johnson's labors than the fact of his prompt adjustment to the plan and mind of God. Education is sometimes disqualification where it ought to be preparation for holy service. Trained scholars sometimes lose childlikeness of spirit and dependence on God, and get proud, self-confident, and lean on their own understanding. The strong are prone to glory in their own strength, the rich in their wealth, the wise in their sagacity, the learned in their knowledge; and so they forget that the only true wisdom, wealth, or glory is in understanding and knowing God. Here was a man so weak, ignorant, poor, obscure, and utterly inadequate for any great achievement, that he had no resource or resort but to trust in Jehovah. He knew he was an earthen vessel, frail and broken, and his only power must be found in a capacity for conveyance of a blessing not his own. Whatever be the reason, the fact is that, as we have seen, he had scarcely begun his work in this worst of all fields when blessing also began to be given.

He had landed at Freetown in April; he had come to Hogbrook in June; on the 14th of July distinct showers of mercy fell on the newly sown seed. Family prayers were held between five and six o'clock in the morning, but, even so early, a throng of natives filled the house. He read and explained the latter part of the forty-sixth chapter of the prophecy of Jeremiah, a passage of Scripture so appropriate to his surroundings and so important as supplying another key to his life-work that we here make prominent the very words upon which his mind was fixed.

> Verse 11: "In vain shalt thou use many medicines;
> For thou shalt not be cured."
> Verse 15: "Why are thy valiant men swept away?
> They stood not,
> Because the Lord did drive them."

Then, the contrast, in verse 27:

> "But fear not thou, O My servant Jacob,
> And be not dismayed, O Israel:
> For, behold, I will save thee from afar off,
> And thy seed from the land of their captivity;
> And Jacob shall return,
> And be in rest and at ease,
> And none shall make him afraid.
> Fear thou not, O Jacob, . . . for I am with thee."

Such was the divine nutriment on which the fainting heart of this simple believer and laborer with God both nourished itself into strength and fed others.

Two hours later that same morning three women were found standing at the door, asking to "learn Book"; and at ten o'clock a service was held, at which Johnson explained the eighteenth chapter of John, dwelling upon the sufferings of Christ as the divine antidote for human sin and sorrow. At this meeting the whole house, and even the piazza and windows, were crowded, and some were obliged to stand in the yard. Then at three o'clock in the afternoon another crowd was addressed on Acts ii. 36, 37:

> "Therefore let all the house of Israel know assuredly, that God hath made that same Jesus, whom ye have crucified, both Lord and Christ. Now when they heard this, they were

pricked in their heart, and said unto Peter and to the rest of the apostles, Men and brethren, what shall we do?"

At this time the throng was too great to be accommodated within range of his voice. And why should it awaken any surprise that God owned a method of dealing with souls that so magnified the Word of His grace, and showed so diligent a search to find the exact medicine whereby the disease of sin should be cured?

Again, at seven o'clock in the evening, a fourth service was held, the house and grounds being filled, and the same old gospel being magnified. And so the work went on from day to day, and from daybreak until far on into the night. He who thus faithfully and tirelessly preached the Word to the multitudes was equally faithful in dealing with individual souls, thus imitating his Master, who spoke to those whom He met by the way, as to the woman at the well.

We have seen how Saturday evenings were set apart for these assemblies for prayer and testimony. Only a few had yet learned how to pray in public, but as the missionary pastor heard them wrestling with God for a blessing, and listened to their simple pleadings and to their touching tales of God's dealings, he experienced such joy as turned that wilderness of Sierra Leone into an Eden, and, like Paul in his rapture to the third heaven, whether he were in the body or out of the body he could not tell. The climate was so unhealthy—the worst in the world—that he felt his time must be short; but, though at times physically prostrate, he could not think of returning to England, and continually blessed God that, at whatever cost of sacrifice, he had been sent by Him on such an errand.

The church building had now become so crowded that the governor of the colony, who frequently attended the services, ordered a gallery built as soon as possible, thus nearly doubling the capacity of the house. And before October one hundred and sixty-four boys were enrolled in the school, upward of twenty pupils were in the family school, and more than fifty adults in the evening classes. We have thus been careful to follow every step and stage of this great work of grace from its beginning, for these were the base-blocks on which that spiritual edifice was reared which still remains almost without a parallel in mission history.

Very marked were the dealings of God with the conscience where an observer might have thought conscience was dead. Early in November Mr. Johnson had written to the Church Missionary Society of several persons who complained of their "bad hearts," and who gave such clear proofs of grace that no one could forbid their baptism, and reference has been already made to their reception as converts. Evidence now accumulated that God's Spirit was at work generally upon the consciences of the Hogbrook slaves, and compelling repentance at cost of much renunciation of sin. Thus, one young man who sought baptism, but was found to be living in sinful relations with a woman, after the loose fashion prevalent in the colony, being rejected, went away with a sad face as though preferring to live in sin; but before the next Sunday he returned, and, sitting down with his face to the wall, gave a striking account of the

Lord's dealing with him. When he was told that he might be baptized and come to the Lord's table only on condition of his marriage with the woman whom he had led into sin, he joyfully consented and at once complied, being married, baptized, and admitted to the Lord's Supper within three hours; and no sooner were these parties married than the wife gave proof that the Spirit was at work also in her heart.

About the same time another encouraging sign appeared. Dr. Macaulay Wilson, who was an attending physician of the negroes and himself also a colored man, after often being an attendant at public worship, came to Johnson, confessing his sin and seeking salvation. He acknowledged that, from the time when he had heard him speak upon the words, "The blood of Jesus Christ His Son cleanseth us from all sin," he had been unable to find rest; that he had often started out purposing to acquaint him with his soul's anxieties, but had by pride been kept back from such confession. Now, however, he made a full acknowledgment of the fact that he had been grievously and notoriously wicked, and asked spiritual counsel. This conversion was an incident of great importance in the history of this mission, for Dr. Wilson was the son of King George of Yongroo, and his accepted heir, and had great influence with the Bullom people. Thus the gospel found its way once more into "Cæsar's household." This colored doctor, this son of the Bullom king, became a very great help and encouragement to Johnson, growing in grace and knowledge of Christ and capacity for service. He acted as clerk on Sunday, and in the absence of the missionary kept the fires burning on the altar of family worship, and himself made most affecting and effective exhortations.

The new gallery was now added to the church, holding two hundred more, and the schools both of children and adults made such progress that as early as February 14, 1817, they were able to report a total of three hundred and thirty scholars.

There were now masons, bricklayers, carpenters, shingle-makers, smiths, sawyers, tailors, and brickmakers connected with the colony, which became after a while a model of thrift and industry.

Smallpox visited the settlement, but the boys and girls were promptly inoculated, as were most of the population, and the only fatal cases in the school were those of two boys and one girl, though several of the people who refused to be inoculated fell victims. The little girl who died gave every reason for confidence that she was a Christian disciple. She lamented very much over her wicked heart, and prayed to Jesus as her only refuge, and was baptized. At her funeral Johnson spoke on Amos iv. 12: "Prepare to meet thy God." She was much beloved by those who knew her, and about three hundred followed the body to the grave, and the occasion made a deep impression. Many of the children at Kissy, however, fell victims to the scourge— above one hundred of them.

Crowds continued to attend family worship, upward of two hundred being habitually present, and sometimes in the evening the church building, though enlarged, was almost full.

It was March 31, 1817, when Johnson was set apart according to the rites of the Lutheran Church, the humble man being not a little distressed by doubts and fears as to his capacity to exercise the functions of an ordained minister; but the Holy Spirit continued so manifestly and abundantly to bless his work that all his questionings were finally silenced. 1 Corinthians i. 25, 26, removed all remaining doubt; or, had any doubt remained, on the following Easter Sunday God set His seal upon this newly ordained minister while speaking to a crowded congregation on John xi. 25, 26. At this time his hearers were so visibly moved that many wept and prayed aloud for mercy. These experiences were repeated precisely in the afternoon, when he spoke on 1 Corinthians xv. 55; and in the evening, while engaged in prayer, crying and praying became so general that he was compelled to leave off and give out a hymn. Even this was of no purpose; he besought them to be still, and gave out another hymn, but was unable to restore quiet; the greater part of the congregation were on their knees crying aloud for pardon. What wonder if Johnson found it impossible to express with tongue or pen the feelings that overcame him, and, like Titus Coan in the work at Hilo and Puna not many years after, he was obliged to leave his congregation in this state, bowed down in tears and cries before God! As he passed toward the door he saw a man on his knees, knocking with his hands on the boards and crying, "Lord Jesus, me no let you go; first pardon my sins." As he went home, quite convinced that God was so dealing with them that he could only leave Him to work, he heard nothing but cries in every direction for the space of about fifteen minutes. He was obliged to use means to prevent further disturbances, for the simple mention of the name of Jesus immediately evoked these outcries; and he gave directions to the doorkeepers that when more than one person was thus affected he must remove such from the building, that the meeting might proceed without disturbance. Strange experiences, indeed, when a minister can keep a service of divine worship sufficiently quiet for himself to be heard only by removing stricken souls from the congregation! Yet so marked were the movings of the Spirit of God that there was seldom a Sunday in which the doorkeepers were not compelled to use such means, that the outcries of a few might not make profit impossible to the many.

The number of communicants had reached seventy before the 1st of March, and the scholars in the school nearly four hundred. The people were so eager to hear the Word of God that on Sundays they came an hour before service to secure a seat, and it became necessary to enlarge the church into a cruciform shape, which nearly doubled the room.

So full of striking incidents is the short career of Johnson at Sierra Leone that the most that can be done is to select some of the more marked examples of the operation of God's grace.

For example, in the daily evening school six men and three women were reading the Testament, and one of the men was asked how he liked his new book. His reply was, "I cannot thank the Lord Jesus enough for this good book, for *I have seen myself in it.*" Unconsciously to himself, he was giving a practical comment upon the words of James, who wrote of him who looketh into the perfect law of liberty, and continueth looking until he seeth what manner of man he is. This humble black man found in the Word of God the magic mirror which reflects every man's character and history and destiny.

And so, every entry in Johnson's journal and every letter he wrote make record of the wonderful workings of God; though he was not without trials of faith and patience, even as Christ forewarned us. His dear wife was so ill that for days she seemed to be dying, though mercifully spared. There were constant accessions to the church of such as were manifestly being saved, and the experiences and inquiries of these simple-minded converts might fill a volume with most fascinating details, all the more interesting because the people had been sunk to such depths of degradation. Johnson noticed one woman who attended morning and evening prayer and was almost always in tears; he thought this strange, as she understood so little English that there seemed to be little chance for the gospel to impress her. On asking her why she wept, she pointed to her heart and said, "Here! here!" She felt like the publican who smote upon his breast as he cried for mercy, as though all possible sin were crowded together there in her own heart. Johnson, as he beheld such scenes, could only recall the promise, "I will work, and who shall let it?" And so plain was God's hand that he could only say, "Lord, carry on the work even as Thou hast begun it."

The community thus being provided with the gospel, this godly man sought to organize it into a more prosperous and harmonious state; and one of his first steps was to start a Benefit Society, the effect of which was greatly to increase the health and happiness, mutual sympathy and harmony, of its members. After a discourse on the goodness of God in sending missionaries to Africa, he suggested that they should form a little society for the relief of their sick members, and that each one of them should subscribe a halfpenny a week. The response was immediate, and one of them said, "Dat be very good t'ing, broders; s'pose one be sick, all be sick; s'pose one be well, all be well"—a very simple but practical comment upon Paul's words in 1 Corinthians xii. 12–27: "Whether one member suffer, all the members suffer with it," etc.

One who had recently been brought out of the depths of sin being asked, "How is your heart now?" replied, "Massa, my heart no live here now, my heart live there," pointing upward. Another, being asked why he wept, said, "God came into my heart, and my heart bad too much, that it made me cry."

Conversion compelled, as everywhere, giving up of idols. Gree-grees, and the like charms or fetishes to which the people cling in their superstitious state, were brought forward and put into the fire, like the occult books of the Ephesian magians.

Already, also, the workman began to find his compensation. When Johnson, partly through illness and overwork, fell at times into depression, God used these simple converts to teach him and comfort his soul. For instance, John Sandy said, "Once me see light, but now me have no light, no peace; my bad heart bring me into all these troubles, and I do not know what I must do; I cannot tell whether I am on the way to hell or heaven." His teacher saw how these simple believers were tried, like himself, with constantly recurring depressions and doubts, and so, whether well or ill, doubting or confident, this indefatigable worker went on with his labors.

His simple methods with these people may be seen by a further illustration. On November 17, 1817, at noon, he spoke to the girls and asked if any of them could tell what they had heard the day before. Hannah Cammel, an usher, said, "I heard you say that if any man, woman, boy, or girl died without Jesus Christ they must go to hell." "What do *you* think, Hannah? Are you with Jesus Christ, or are you without Him?" "I am without Him, sir." "Did you ever pray to Him?" "Yes, sir." "Why or what for did you pray to Him?" "To save me from my sins, sir." "Do you know what Jesus Christ did for sinners?" "He came into the world to save them, sir." "Well, then, if He came into the world to save sinners, and you say you are a sinner, He came to save you." She appeared so affected by this truth that she could speak no more.

We have before referred to those seductive snares of fetish-worshipers known as gree-grees. On September 10, 1818, a man from Cockle Bay came into town offering these things for sale, and was brought to Johnson as a sort of malefactor. The missionary reminded his captors and accusers that such were some of them, not long before in the same darkness of superstition, and taught them to pity rather than to despise and hastily judge and condemn the evil-doer; then, quietly turning to the vender of these devil's wares, he counseled him not to come to Regent's Town with his worthless trash, but, if he would persist in such business, to seek some better market.

About an hour later a whole box of gree-grees was brought in, some of which were both rare and valuable, such as even Johnson had never before seen; but these boys and girls, like the converts of Ephesus again, with great joy and acclamations committed them to the flames.

Thus, to this praying man was committed the power to open the windows of heaven; and the cloud which at first was no bigger than a man's hand had already overspread the whole sky, and there was a sound of abundance of rain in the moral desert of Sierra Leone.

CHAPTER V

FIRST-FRUITS UNTO GOD

THAT devout man who is the founder of the China Inland Mission has well reminded us that, though Satan, the hinderer, may "build a hedge about us" to restrain our holy activity, he cannot "roof us in and keep us from looking up." Nothing need prevent a child of God from praying, and praying always brings every other best blessing.

Elijah "prayed, and the heavens gave rain, and the earth brought forth her fruit." That is a typical history of all true revivals or refreshings from on high. Some one has prayed, and showers of blessing always descend when prayers ascend. Johnson knew how to pray, and his spirit of intercession and supplication proved contagious in Sierra Leone, so that even these slaves at Hogbrook learned to prevail with God. Among the first-fruits of faithful gospel teaching was this boldness in coming to the throne of grace. Early in the morning, while it was yet dark, January 15, 1818, Johnson was awakened by hearing from some distance the sound of prayer. He rose and went out on the veranda, but could distinguish only a few words until, the prayer being ended, a number of voices blending in sacred song, he heard the familiar doxology:

"To Father, Son, and Holy Ghost."

Then followed another prayer, loud and clear enough to be distinguished as the voice of a lad, who for ten or twelve minutes poured out his very soul before God, somewhat thus:

"Lord Jesus, my heart too bad, bad too much. Me want to love you, me want to serve you; bad heart not let me. O Lord Jesus, me can't make me good. Take away bad heart; give me new heart. Me sin every day; pardon my sin. O Lord Jesus, make me sin no more."

There were other prayers, whose utterances

were not so distinct, but in them all the name of Jesus was as ointment poured forth. These young seekers after God were holding a meeting by moonlight, for as yet it had not dawned, and, like the psalmist, they with their prayers and praises "prevented the dawning of the morning."

With emotions that found vent only in sobs and tears, their pastor went back to bed, but not to sleep. Overawed and overwhelmed, a holy excitement forbade slumber. In those sounds of prayer he had heard the footfalls of God,—the sound of a rushing, mighty wind from heaven, precursor of a new Pentecost,—and he was prepared for new and more vivid signs that God was nigh, at the very doors. He was in that strange, unearthly mood of expectancy when one waits in silent, speechless awe for greater and more general manifestations of the Holy Spirit's presence, and knowing not what form they may assume, can only hush his own breathing.

Of course such an expectant spirit is never disappointed. Diligent inquiry failed to disclose who they were that he had overheard engaged in this moonlight meeting, but three days later, at the morning service, during prayer, a number of persons present were overtaken with a suspicious drowsiness. Observing this, the missionary gently cautioned his hearers to beware of sluggish habits of praying, reminding them that it is not the formal, listless petition that God hears, but such asking as engages the whole heart and is spiritually earnest. As he pressed the matter upon the consciences of such as had been sleeping while others were praying, several cried aloud, and such confusion was created by those who were thus overcome of emotion that a hymn was sung while the doorkeepers removed them. Trembling and unable to walk or even stand, they had to be carried out literally, in the arms of others, before sufficient quiet was restored.

These violent ebullitions of feeling became common occurrences, and sometimes occasioned harsh criticism on the part of refined people who witnessed or heard of them. But those who have studied the history of revivals well know that such manifestations have often been connected with undoubted and marked movements of the Spirit. Such occasional violent outbreaks of emotion we cannot afford to despise as hypocritical or denounce as artificial and hysterical. Periods of spiritual awakening have too often been attended by such physical phenomena for us to pass harsh and hasty judgments upon them. Very notably, in the Hawaiian Islands a quarter of a century later, and in Ireland half a century later, similar signs followed. At Hilo and Puna, Titus Coan, as we have before hinted, had frequently to stop preaching, praying, and even singing, while he beheld a vast congregation of five thousand so broken down with contrition for sin that scores and hundreds of them fainted and fell to the ground in a swoon.

Like Mr. Coan after him, Johnson did nothing either to excite or to encourage such excessive emotion, but, in fact, rather sought to suppress such outbursts, speaking against them as unseemly interruptions; but he found that the most he could do was to moderate or modify what neither he nor his hearers were able to control or suppress. Asa Mahan, Charles G. Finney, Henry Grattan Guinness, and others who have witnessed these cyclonic storms of feeling, like Mr. Coan and Mr. Johnson, became satisfied at last that in some mysterious way they were due to, or at least connected with, the Spirit's work. No man long engages in successful evangelistic labors without learning that the Holy Spirit of God, like the wind, bloweth where and as He listeth, and we hear the sound thereof—sometimes a gentle murmur or soft zephyr, sometimes a hurricane roar or a tornado blast, but, whether in whispers or in thunders, alike mysterious, divine, independent of man, uncontrollable by man, inexplicable to man.

There is another law of revivals which Johnson found at work in Regent's Town. Whenever and wherever the Spirit of God is supernaturally and marvelously working, the spirits of evil are doubly active, so that a decided outburst of genuine religious life is commonly the signal for an outbreak of scandalous sin. Mr. Kelly, the schoolmaster, had to be dismissed and sent back in disgrace to Freetown, the governor so fully approving Mr. Johnson's course in the matter that he determined no longer to employ Mr. Kelly in any capacity. Besides this serious drawback, the African fever, which has been the great foe of missions to the Dark Continent and so fatal to hundreds of workers, again laid Mr. Johnson prostrate; in fact, his symptoms were alarming; but his life was spared.

As he was beginning to rally from this attack of illness, a woman applied for baptism who had already done so a score of times. She could only say, in the broken dialect that became so precious as the vehicle of the Spirit, "My bad heart follow me all the time; me can't do no good—heart too bad—will not let me. Me want to serve Jesus, but me no sabby how [know how], me too much 'fraid. Suppose me die? Me go to fire—me been bad too much." When asked what she meant by her bad heart following her always, her reply was, "Me no want to do bad, but me heart always do want to do bad, and so follow me always."

In a few cases the simple utterances of these ignorant negroes are here recorded, partly because they give completeness to the narrative, partly because they lend vividness to the portraiture, and partly because in this very absence of the more refined and cultured forms of expression we have an additional proof of genuineness. Obviously we detect here no traces of the stereotyped phrases of the church catechism or the theological system. This is simply the dialect of the universal man. In the seventh chapter of the Epistle to the Romans we have the same confession in substance, only framed in more elegant language: "For that which I do I allow not: for what I would, that do I not; but what I hate, that do I. . . . The evil which I would not, that I do. . . . I see another law in my members, warring against the law of my mind, and bringing me into captivity to the law of sin."

Here is one of the evidences of Christianity: from pole to pole, from sunrise to sunset, whatever be the clime, color, class, or caste, wherever the gospel reaches and touches human souls the results are essentially the same. In the mirror of the divine Word and Spirit heart answers to heart, as in water face answereth to face. Both in sin and in salvation there is one common experience, however variously expressed.

Even at the early stage of Mr. Johnson's ministry at Regent's Town other tokens of divine co-working were not wanting. Conviction of sin was wrought, not in open transgressors only, but in converted men and women, who saw and lamented their coldness and indifference, became acutely and painfully sensible of their inconsistencies and deficiencies, and yearned for more holiness and usefulness. The public services were so thronged that it became necessary to remove a partition wall and so again double the seating capacity, but the audience-room was no sooner enlarged than it was again filled.

Deep conviction of sin and contrition for sin were so common as to be quite general, and one instance must suffice as representative of many, for every day was full of like incidents, and history was making fast.

Hannah Cammel, the usher in the girls' school, who now gave such evidence of regeneration that Johnson could not hesitate about receiving her into membership, had previously such deep distress on account of her sins that she declared that she had no rest day nor night. Like the psalmist, she felt her iniquities too many for her, and she could not look up. She actually believed herself the "chief of sinners." Her patient teacher could only turn her eyes to Him who came to seek and to save that which was lost, and pray that the same divine Spirit who had shown her her great sins would also show her the great Sin-bearer. Only He who pricks the heart until we cry, "What shall I do?" can withdraw His sharp arrow, and in withdrawing it leave behind in the wounded conscience His soothing salve, the Balm of Gilead.

As Johnson watched God's wonder-working among these debased and degraded tribes, he marveled anew at the grace that touches all sinners alike, imparts essentially the same experience of salvation to all, and makes the same fruits of faith and love to grow in all.

This devoted servant of God found that even saints have to wrestle against principalities and powers. Trials and temptations seemed to multiply and intensify in proportion as "flesh and blood" seemed subdued or the Spirit's work became deeper rooted and wider spread.

For instance, one of his communicants was determined to marry an unconverted girl, and he felt constrained to oppose it, and quoted to him the divine injunction, "Be not unequally yoked together with unbelievers," and bade him pray much before taking such a step. But, being in no mood to accept such advice, his passion's fires quite swept away both his sound judgment and his self-control, and he angrily demanded that Mr. Johnson should perform the ceremony. Too conscientious to be a party to what he regarded as an unscriptural union, the patient pastor remonstrated, but in vain. The man bade him erase his name from the church roll, as he would no longer have anything to do with either church or pastor.

The tender-hearted missionary was greatly

grieved, lest the whole affair should become known and prove a public scandal and disgrace. When persuaded still to attend family prayer by William Tamba, one of Johnson's helpers, the man's face exhibited such hardness and wore such a diabolical expression that many observed and spoke of it. At the same time some idle women, who, though communicants, were busybodies in other men's matters, were going from house to house, peddling gossip and speaking things they ought not. There was also a quarrel between a man and his wife, leading to blows, and caused by a slanderous report which had reached his ears that she was going about from house to house while he was at work.

Poor Johnson! his head was as waters and his eyes a fountain of tears, for he wept day and night, as he beheld one of Christ's disciples, who had been much beloved, aflame with an unholy passion and apostatizing for its sake; another beating his own wife in unjust anger, and idle slanderers, whose tongues were set on fire of hell, kindling heartburnings in peaceful homes.

He who awhile before could not sleep for joy, now could not for grief and anxiety. All this vicarious sorrow and caretaking induced morbid spiritual states, so that at times he began to doubt the genuineness of his converts, and even his own saved state. The moment the devil finds a disciple dropping his shield of faith, he is more than ready with his fiery darts. This servant of God got disheartened, and so distrustful. "Are these people all hypocrites?" he asked, "and am I one myself? All my past feelings and experiences seem at times but my own imaginings or a delusive dream."

There is a comfort, after all, in human frailty. "Elijah was a man of like passions as we are;" that prince of God, who prevailed to open and shut heaven's flood-gates, was but a man like ourselves. Even Jesus Himself had His hours of deep darkness, as in Gethsemane and the crisis of atonement on Calvary. The Book of Psalms is given to disciples as a mirror of universal experience: every child of God sees himself reflected there, and every possible mood and frame of joy or sorrow, hope or despair, ecstasy or apathy, finds there both a response and, if need be, a remedy. It is a harp of a thousand strings, and any chords of feeling that vibrate in our experience may be heard by him who listens to the dirges, plaints, wails, or anthems and choral shouts of the inspired psalmist.

If Johnson, like other men, turned at times toward the darkness, he always returned to the true Light. A faithful biographical sketch, like a true portrait, leaves out nothing; even the infirmities and sins of God's people have their lesson. This man of God, blessed in his work for souls as few others have ever been, was subject to like temptations as others. His prayers brought down copious rains after long drought, and yet he was made after the frail human pattern. Saints are perfect only as they are perfect in Christ Jesus.

His sermons were a sort of journal indexing his mental states and reflecting his spiritual habits. About this time he preached on Matthew xiv. 12: "And went and told Jesus." It was because the dove of his own heart, circling over restless waters and finding no perch, in its farthest flight never quite lost sight of the ark, and was still under its attraction and sway, that it invariably fluttered back to God's bosom. He went and told Jesus, and so he taught his people to go, like John's sorrowing disciples, and pour their complaints and anxieties into the Master's ear.

If some of his converts gave him anxiety, others bore unmistakable fruits of the Spirit. When William Tamba lost by death a bullock and a goat, which constituted the bulk of his worldly estate, he only said, like Job, "He that gave them took them away," and under his heavy losses seemed so cheerful that his joy in God was more marked in his adversity than in his prosperity, and made a singular impression on all who knew him.

The simple and broken utterances of these untaught children of the Dark Continent were so touching and so striking that their pastor wrote many of them down in his journal. Some of them are worthy of preservation as part of this wonderful story of missions.

"Me heart too much trouble—sometimes so hard, will not let me pray. Hope the Lord Jesus teach me more and more to love Him and serve Him. I poor guilty sinner; thank God, He send Jesus to save me, poor sinner."

"Me heart remember all them bad things me do before; me bad too much."

"Wicked things trouble me too much; me want to do good, but wicked heart no let me. Me heart run awa [about] all this week. Suppose me pray, me heart run to my country —all about. Sometimes them things me no want to remember more come into my heart, and then me can't say any more but, 'Jesus, have mercy on me, poor thing.' Me no sabby [know] what me must do—hope Jesus save me. Suppose He no save me, me lost forever."

"Sometimes you preach, massa, me t'ink you talk only to me. Me say in heart, 'That me!' Me been do that thing. Sometimes me t'ink me have two hearts*—one want do good, other always want do bad. O Jesus, have mercy on poor sinner."

* Compare Rom. vii.

"My husband he no pray, no serve God. Suppose me talk to him about God palaver [preaching], he take whip, he flog me. Me have trouble much, but Jesus help me take all the trouble."

Missionaries, and other visitors at Regent's Town, attending public services of worship, saw the church filled with from one thousand to twelve hundred black people, their faces lit up with eager desire after the Word, and among the converts some from the Ebo nation and other tribes, the most savage and brutal that were found in the slave-vessels; and they were compelled to declare that nothing less than a miracle had been wrought in the mission. Moreover, these very converts, themselves just plucked as brands from the burning, and having the smell of fire and the smutch of the burning brand yet on them, crowded the church on the first Monday of the month, at the missionary concert, planning for the rescue of others yet in the fire of sin, and bringing forward their contributions, a willing offering.

With a refuse population like this to deal with, it was like bringing the order and beauty of cosmos out of chaos to develop holy living, and the perversity and depravity of evil were repeatedly exhibited.

In the school there were outbreaks of ungovernable temper. One day the largest but one of the girls, and the most tiresomely headstrong, not only refused to obey the head usher, but caught hold of her and beat her. The assault was renewed after an interval, and so Johnson had to interfere. The case called for sharp discipline, and he took the whip and laid a few strokes on the back of the rebellious scholar. The lash caught on some obstacle, and rebounding struck his own left eye, which was instantly covered with blood. The pain was so great as to induce faintness and sickness, and for three days both eyes were nearly blind. The affliction only served to bring out the deep love of these poor negroes for Johnson, whom they constantly visited and for whom they showed the solicitude of devotion. Some, whose piety and sincerity he had doubted, thus proved both the reality of their faith in Christ and of their love toward His servant, and so again all things worked together for good.

Mr. Johnson's narrative abounds in references to the surprisingly untiring attendance of these converts upon the so-called "means of grace." There were people, and not a few, who attended every Sunday six separate services of worship, beginning with a prayer-meeting at six o'clock in the morning, then a preaching service at half-past ten, another prayer-meeting at two o'clock, another preaching service at three, and concluding the day with two more prayer-meetings at six and a quarter past eight. And distance was no obstacle, nor was an inconvenient, uncomfortable state of weather. The Word of God laid hold on them; they learned that God is a prayer-hearer, and they came as those who expected to get blessing, and were never disappointed. Here was an apostolic church like unto the primitive assemblies, springing up on African soil and producing all the early fruits of faith and godliness. Truly God is no respecter of persons. Who shall ever measure the possibilities of grace when such astonishing results appear on such a field as first-fruits unto God?

CHAPTER VI

FLOODS UPON THE DRY GROUND

THE history of missions is the standing witness and irresistible proof of the fact that God is, and is a rewarder of those who diligently seek Him. The story of these seven years in Sierra Leone is itself another burning bush, which, although it grew in a desert, exhibits every leaf and twig aflame with the divine presence; and to this day no one who looks intently upon it can help exclaiming, "How wonderful is it!"

Yet in all this experience of God's working there was perpetual need of man's watching. The missionary found, both in himself and in his surroundings, abundant occasion for unceasing prayerfulness and watchfulness. He himself was but human, and full of the follies and frailties of a fallen man; a moment of self-confidence or self-dependence might betray him not only into grievous mistakes, but into serious sins and departures from the living God. There were European residents in the colony who vigorously believed nothing and consistently practised what they believed, exhibiting their creed in their conduct; and there were also formalists and ritualists, who had neither any true conception of spiritual worship nor any real insight into the inner meaning and purport of divine ordinances. Nor could there be any doubt of a personal devil, nor of his mighty working; for he seemed to have come down, having great wrath, as though he knew that his time was short, and was determined to work all the havoc and ruin possible in this rapidly transforming community.

It was the habit of Johnson not to spare himself. Perhaps he often went to an extreme in his exertions and was unduly careless of health. Those who, like him, find themselves confronting a whole multitude of most debased and depraved humanity, in perishing need of help for both body and soul, and yet compelled to minister to such complex misery and poverty single-handed, have often sacrificed themselves in the vain attempt to overtake the destitution and degradation about them. Ordinary prudence is forgotten in passion for souls; the barriers of conscious self-preservation are often swept away by the resistless impulse of love for dying men. The maxims of health, the imperative laws of rest and recreation, the demand for pure air, good food, abundant sleep, are not so much forgotten as disregarded in the multiplying activities of a man who sees no way of escape from crowded meetings, ceaseless labors, unwholesome diet, and broken rest, except in the utter abandonment of his work.

This may be indefensible and even suicidal, but it is an experience which is so common with the most devoted servants of God that it cannot easily be remedied. Our blessed Lord Himself found no leisure so much as to eat, and had to take the night and the lonely mountain-top to find a time and place for prayerful communion with God. The question asked Him by controversial Jews, "Thou art not yet fifty years old, and hast Thou seen Abraham?" hints that the young man of thirty may have presented the appearance of premature age, as though twenty years older, because of the too rapid expenditure of vitality in the unavoidable pressure of His ministry to souls and bodies.

Whatever be the ethics of Mr. Johnson's case, the fact is that more than once he rose from a sick-bed, weak and exhausted, to go to his pulpit or prayer-meeting, lest his hungry flock should go untended or unfed. Sometimes, like Lyman Beecher, he found a good "pulpit sweat" acting as a tonic and stimulant, but there were too many cases in which such exertions were far from remedial.

From these aspects of his work, and experience of weakness and conflict, we turn, however, to the singular and almost unprecedented success which so abundantly repaid all expenditure of time and strength that all self-loss was more than forgotten in the vast gains of others. If he had ever for a moment doubted the divine vitality of which the gospel was the hiding, he could not question that in this seed of the Word there lay the secret of all wisdom and power. He saw that seed, sown by himself in a soil as hopeless as any in the wide world field, actually taking root, and not only taking root, but bearing fruit—the same fruit as elsewhere and in the most promising soil. Plants of godliness, trees of righteousness, were growing rapidly and already stood there in Regent's Town, proving God's own husbandry, and men were constrained to call them the planting of the Lord, that He might be glorified.*

Every day was fraught with events that go to make history. For example, on November 27, 1817, he visited King George of Yongroo, in the Bullom settlement, and as he observed the devils' houses and the influence of the gree-grees, he could only thank God for the contrast to all this presented at Hogbrook. On his return he was welcomed with such enthusiasm that he could get no farther than his door, both house and piazza being

* Isaiah lxi. 3.

thronged, and from that point he addressed the crowd. At an evening meeting he read an anecdote of a poor woman who had, at cost of much sacrifice, contributed to missions; and when he had done speaking four communicants spoke in behalf of the cause of missions, and asked to form a missionary society, and urged that one evening each week might be set apart for its meetings. December 3d being designated, at seven o'clock the church building was full. A service of prayer had preceded, as nothing was done without first counseling with God; and a brief talk followed, in which Mr. Johnson, referring to their former state without Christ, depicted the misery of the heathen, and urged them both to send out and support their own missionary, and encouraged them to bring their own little gifts, by commenting on Mark xii. 42-44, the story of the widow and her two mites. No less than seventeen converts followed him, speaking much to the purpose, although in broken English, and their pastor wished in his heart that friends in England might have heard those simple exhortations. William Tamba prayed

God to send out more laborers to the regions beyond, and emphasized both his prayer and his speech by giving a half-crown. Thinking that he might not understand that a monthly offering was contemplated, it was so explained to him; but his answer was, "I know, and I will give a similar sum each month." Several others followed his example. It was then decided that those who became members should undertake to give not less than twopence a month, and one hundred and seven at once became subscribers, after which several of the school-boys and -girls gave their pence and halfpence. One boy, being asked where he had got his money, answered, "Me have three coppers [i.e., halfpence] long time; me beg massa take two, me keep one." Mr. Johnson advised him to keep them all, but he insisted that at least two should be put in the mission fund, which deeply stirred the heart of his pastor.

The next day after the formation of this missionary society it was announced that a visit was to be made to Leicester Mountain in the evening, where all the missionaries were to meet to pray for the spread of the gospel, and that any who wished to accompany Mr. Johnson must be ready at four o'clock, dressed and clean. Three hundred and twenty-one went with him. It seemed incredible, even to the missionary himself, that all these his companions had so short a time before seemed almost beyond the reach of grace.

The large place of meeting was filled, and some were standing in the yard. It was an occasion never to be forgotten, and as they marched back they sang with joy such hymns as:

> "How beauteous are their feet,
> Who stand on Zion's hill;
> Who bring salvation on their tongues,
> And words of peace reveal!"

The following Lord's day afternoon the sacramental Supper was administered to some eighty persons, Mr. Cates making the address; but when about half through his remarks he was suddenly overtaken by fever, and had to leave Mr. Johnson to complete the discourse; who also, though he had finished the sermon, was prostrated by fever, so that the people had to take charge of the evening service themselves. The next day Mr. Johnson's symptoms were alarmingly violent, for he became delirious; but a messenger, hastily despatched to the governor, returned with a physician mounted on horseback, and his recovery was rapid. One such glimpse at both the work and its hindrances may suffice, for it is a fair example of experiences extended through seven years.

Physical transformations were also wrought by the gospel. In place of desolation and devastation, Johnson, in 1818, surveying Regent's Town from a high rock, could see the prophecy in Isaiah xxxv. 1, 2 literally fulfilled. What in 1816 was a desert overgrown with bush, and the dwelling-place of wild men and wild beasts, was two years later a fruitful field, garden spots, fields covered with rice, cocoa, cassavas, yams, plantains, and bananas. With a joy that to be known must be felt, he saw the vilest vices and most abhorrent practices give place to habits of industry and virtue, and practical morality and piety manifested in the daily life of hundreds of people. Promiscuous concubinage would be too refined a phrase for the nameless enormities which had prevailed and which were now supplanted and displaced by honorable marriage and domestic purity. When, on July 5, 1818, he united in holy wedlock James Bell, a stone-mason, and Hannah Cammel, an usher in the girls' school, both of them communicants in his church and wearing European dress, he regarded it as marking a new epoch in the mission. This was the finest black couple he had ever united in matrimony; they represented the fruits of such civilization as the gospel produces, and he felt a holy pride in contemplating such a basis for a Christian home and household amid the pagan darkness of Africa.

Family life is another sphere which severely tests the genuineness and depth of the work of grace, and here again gospel triumphs were made conspicuous. Under sin's reign we sometimes see a whole people perishing by excess of deaths over births, while even the births themselves are largely the fruit of crime.

At Sierra Leone in one day in 1816 more persons died than were born during a whole year, for there were seven deaths daily and but six births in the three hundred and sixty-five. Two years later it was recorded that within six months only seven deaths had occurred, while forty-two were born, and the excess was therefore already fivefold.

In 1817 a mutual Benefit Society was organized, consisting of communicants only, each member paying a halfpenny per week, thus forming a fund from which to supply help in sickness or other times of need. This proved a conspicuous means of promoting and fostering unselfish love and mutual harmony. It was another of the fruits of godliness, for every one learned to look, not on his own things solely, but on the things of others. These new converts thus early thought of and cared for one another. And though they were so poor, the half-yearly contributions from January to June, 1818, reached in halfpence nearly seven pounds sterling.

These converted blacks were faithful church-goers, not easily kept away by the weather. Through torrents of rain they trudged over roads ankle-deep in mud, and forded streams sometimes up to the waist, and even to the neck, that they might worship God. Nearly two years after Johnson began labors among them he put on record in his journal that "not one service had been neglected" since he came there. During the rainy season, when the overflow of the streams submerged even the bridges, the people waded through the water up to the armpits rather than be deprived of such privileges, and thus, whether rainy or fair, the house of prayer was always full.

When, for any cause, these simple-minded converts were kept from the missionary prayer service, they came afterward to bring their small offerings, thus showing more self-sacrifice and zeal than many a more enlightened disciple, who acts as though to escape a "collection" were simply so much saved!

The fruits of faith are not easily counterfeited even by that master of frauds, the devil. Systematic and cheerful giving may be counted among the remarkable signs of grace. Paul, in that great essay on Christian giving which occupies the eighth and ninth chapters of Second Corinthians, presents an example so rare that even yet it has few parallels. Those Macedonian disciples were so glad to give that, when their deep poverty made him feel reluctant to accept their offerings, they, with much entreaty, begged him to receive their gift and admit them to the sacred privilege and fellowship of this ministry to poor saints of the Lord.

It was given to these Regent's Town converts to imitate these Macedonians in their eagerness to give. One morning some brought money due for the following month's contribution to missions, and when the inquiry was naturally made as to the reason for this advance payment, the explanation of one was: "I may be sick next month and unable to pay, so I pay now to make sure!"

We now come to a time in the history of this work when the floods of water were poured upon the dry ground, and the blessing was so abundant and enriching that even the minute features of the narrative acquire fascinating interest. Nothing seems insignificant when God mightily moves among men. We may well give close attention to details, lest we lose some part of the significance of this pentecostal outpouring.

On September 6, 1818, the church was so densely thronged that even the vestry, gallery stairs, tower, and windows were full, and some of the extra seats broke down with their burden. When pastor Johnson came in and looked on the eager throng, his heart was so full both of joy and of awe that he could scarcely restrain his emotion or open his mouth in controlled speech. The groanings and loud cries were more rare, but in their place there was a holy silence as in the presence of God.

After the service he observed boys and girls going into a field, and he went up to the housetop to watch them. Shortly they parted, the boys going one way and the girls another, and at length he could see them all kneeling behind different clumps of bushes for prayer. When the evening service was over, the boys sought him and told him how they had been out in the field to pray, but found that they did not know how. They said they had heard that Jesus prayed for them, and would like to know if that were really true. He then in simple words explained to them the office of the great High Priest and Intercessor at God's right hand, and they went again to the field, joyfully to resume praying. It was a bright, still, moonlight night, and the scene was awfully impressive. Groups of girls could be seen here in one part of the field, and there, at some little distance off upon a high rock, the boys were gathered. Through the quiet night air their voices were clearly heard repeating and then singing hymns, and engaging in prayer, and their words could almost be distinguished. Many of the older people, hearing, arose and went to join these "infant congregations," where, as out of the mouth of babes and sucklings, God was once more perfecting His praise.

Next morning Johnson awoke early, hearing the girls behind the school-house singing and praying; and his wife advised their going back to bed, lest others should be disturbed. Shortly after, about four o'clock, the boys were heard singing in their houses, and word was sent to them likewise to keep silence and not to wake those who needed sleep. But who could doubt that a power from above was at work among the schoolchildren of Regent's Town?

The morning signal rang for family worship, but it was raining so hard, and the wind blowing so like a tornado, that few were expected to morning prayers. Imagine the surprise when, looking from his window, the missionary saw the streets thronged, and going into the large church found it as full as on Sunday! Mr. Davis and Tamba had been with the boys until two o'clock in the morning, and testified that they could not have believed mere lads capable of such gifts in prayer. All the people seemed to be breathing a heavenly air and bathed in the light of God. Their whole conversation was in heaven, and seemed an illustration of what is recorded of Elijah, that he *stood* in the presence of Jehovah.

Outsiders who ventured within could not fail to recognize an unusual but indefinable solemnity that pervaded these assemblies. A carpenter from Leopold's Town begged that permission might be obtained from the governor for him to stay at Regent's Town, so reluctant was he to get out of the circle where such blessing abode.

Just before Mr. Johnson retired for rest September 7, 1818, the girls asked if they might not go into the church to sing and pray. Permission was given, with the condition that but two hymns should be sung, in order to allow others to sleep. But the singing had only begun when *all the people who heard it got up and joined them*. Johnson's own servant, Mary Wynah, was the first to pray, and not a man or boy was then present, but when her prayer was concluded the boys, who had come in, took up the supplication, and the prayers continued until six o'clock in the morning, when the throng reluctantly dispersed and went quietly to bed.

The next day, after school, boys and girls together again resorted to the church for prayer, while the missionary and his wife, standing behind the window or sitting under the staircase, drank in delight as they heard these little ones pour out their hearts to God. At last the prayer of a boy but ten years old was so marvelously rich in spiritual experience that the heart of the missionary burst with emotion. He could stay no longer without crying aloud, and, with full soul and streaming eyes, he sought some place where he could give free vent to his pent-up feelings. Even then he could scarcely pray in words, for tears choked his utterance, and he could only cry, amid sobs of joy, "O my God and Saviour, what hast Thou done! What shall I render to Thee?"

Such rejoicing was not, however, unmingled with trembling. He was overawed at such clear signs of the divine presence, but he had observed that whenever the Spirit of holiness was peculiarly active the spirits of evil redoubled their activity also, and such continued to be his experience to the very end of his life. Johnson remarked, "I am afraid the devil will roar very loud hereafter," reminding one of the Cornish miner and evangelist, Billy Bray, who always counted on Satan's making a special row whenever the spirit of revival broke out among the people, and braced himself for the encounter.

The attachment of these young converts to their missionary pastor was wonderful in both strength and tenderness. For instance, when Mr. Garnon died, the governor wished Mr. Johnson to hold service at Freetown, August 2, 1818. When it was known that he was going to comply, his whole parish was in an uproar of excitement lest he should stay at Freetown to take Mr. Garnon's place, and he could with difficulty pacify his people even by the most emphatic assurances of his return. They declared that if he changed his field of residence and labor they all would follow in a body; and when at last he prevailed on them to consent to his going for the Sunday, they declared that if he did not come back promptly on Monday they would go and fetch him!

His experience at Freetown was not such as would be likely to wean him from his devoted flock. He found a motley congregation, in which were the governor and some officers, together with soldiers and the inhabitants of the town. He spoke from Acts xix. 2, but the Word fell on very unfruitful soil. Indeed, a spirit not only of lethargy, but of levity, pervaded the assembly. He was annoyed by the laughter of the officers, who seemed on the point of leaving in the midst of the meeting, and one did go out. The audience generally were as uninterested and inattentive as though blind and deaf, and the black soldiers were apparently the only ones who inclined to give the preacher a decent hearing. When at noon he reached home, he felt himself not only in another atmosphere, but in a new world. Some of the people, in their impatience for his return, met him on the hill as he approached, and he found Dr. Macaulay Wilson's house crowded, with preparations for keeping the Lord's Supper. In the evening he addressed a throng that seemed to drink in every word he spoke, and again he thanked God for such proofs of His presence, and for a people whose hearts were not closed and hardened against the truth.

Not only were they good hearers and not forgetful, but they were doers of the work. They heard for a practical purpose. For instance, finding a dispute existing among his church-members, he at once preached from Luke vi. 37: "Forgive, and ye shall be forgiven." The Word had immediate effect. Before they left the house all the disputants had confessed to one another with sorrow their misdoings and their desire for peace. Harmony was at once restored. The house of God became the gate of heaven once more, opening into love's fragrant gardens.

In August, 1818, nine of the sixteen applicants for baptism were school-girls, and in the cases of some of them their youth was a ground of hesitancy. But they gave proofs so simple, yet so ample and striking, of the working of God's grace in their minds and hearts, that their pastor dared not refuse them. Among them was one, a girl of eleven, whom his wife two years before had taken into their home and named Hagar Johnson. He was strongly opposed to her joining the church, yet he could find nothing to blame in her conduct, and at her examination as to the evidence of her regenerate state this mere child of eleven years gave an account of her experience of grace so satisfactory that it is not irreverent to apply to her such words as were written of her Master when he was twelve years of age: all that heard her were astonished at her understanding and answers. Mr. Johnson's objections were swept away, and she was received. Nor had he any occasion to regret it, for he often found this young disciple on her knees, praying and weeping as she yearned after God, or, like some mature saint, visiting the fatherless and widows in their affliction, ministering to the sick and the needy, while she never failed to show piety at home.

The Spirit used the Word as the sword, the hammer, and the fire, all at once. The most hardened and hostile were pricked in their hearts, broken into contrition, melted into obedience. Those who had been most hopelessly bound by habits of sin found their fetters broken, their prison doors opened, and themselves free. It was the acceptable year of the Lord. On one occasion, the greatest enemy of the missionary and his message, who had in every way fought against the truth, working all uncleanness with greediness, came to Mr. Johnson in the greatest distress of mind for guidance.

The numbers of those who manifested desire after godliness were at times so great that the testimony of his own eyes could scarcely be believed. It was more like an illusive dream than a sober reality. Yet it could be no dream, for as he closely observed he saw how the whole conduct and character, thought and utterance, had undergone a transformation.

How great was the joy of these Sierra Leone converts in their newly found Saviour may be seen by the praise they publicly gave to God that they had ever *been sold into slavery*, since their bondage to man had been the means used in His providence for introducing them into the liberty of the Lord's freemen.

Early in his experiences at Hogbrook, Mr. Johnson records his manner of studying God's Word, which should be embodied in this narrative as both important and instructive, and of permanent value as revealing secrets of his success. His humility and self-distrust drove him to find all sufficiency in God, and his testimony is unequivocal:

"I have learned by experience that when I have studied a passage, divided and subdivided it, and am thus well prepared by my own imaginations, I feel no power to explain it; but that when I entirely lean upon God the Holy Spirit's influence, and thus begin, divisions and subdivisions come flowing apace."

His constant prayer was that whenever, in the name of Jesus, he stood up, he might entirely depend on the wisdom that comes from above. And it must be confessed that the simple sermons which he preached evinced much of the Spirit's teaching, even if they were not framed on the best homiletic models.

For example, let us take, almost at random, an outline on Isaiah lxii. 12: "1. The election: God's people a 'holy people.' 2. Their redemption: 'Redeemed of the Lord.' 3. Their calling: 'Sought out.' 4. Their final perseverance: 'A city not forsaken.'"

CHAPTER VII

THE REGIONS BEYOND

THERE are two passions that rank highest among all those impulsive, propulsive forces which can control a human soul. One is the passion for God, and the other is the passion for men. These are companion gifts and graces, representing the noblest, divinest affections of which in our best estate we are capable, and are correspondingly difficult for even Satan, the master counterfeiter, to imitate.

By passion for God is meant that unutterable yearning after the divine nature and holiness which our Lord expresses by hunger and thirst after righteousness, and which led to Tholuck's famous declaration: "I have but one passion, and it is He, it is He!" By passion for men is meant that kindred love for souls which leads to earnest, self-denying labors for the salvation of men as such, irrespective of rank, place, caste, class, color, or condition.

Samuel J. Mills so yearned over earth's perishing multitudes that even the vast valley of the Mississippi was to him "like a pinhole," and he felt a sense of restraint and limitation even within the entire territory of the United States, vast as it was. And so Johnson felt "like a bird in a cage" in Sierra Leone, beating the wings of his holy aspiration against the bars that kept him from a larger flight. He would gladly have been as free as the apocalyptic angel flying through the midst of heaven with the everlasting gospel. His mind was constantly wandering into the regions beyond, and many a night was spent in sleepless, restless yearnings and praying for the Dark Continent as a whole. He, like Coleridge, saw life in two aspects:

> "The petty done,
> The undone vast."

His passion for souls only revealed to him his comparative apathy and lethargy—a common phenomenon that still perplexes and torments many of the best of God's saints. Growth in the likeness of Christ serves only to make us seem to ourselves further from the complete image of His perfection. One very marked peculiarity of Johnson was his mercurial temperament, and this must always be borne in mind in following the course of his life-story. The territory through which a stream runs determines the residuum which it leaves on its bed, whether it be gold or red oxide of iron and green sulphur. It is an encouragement to others who find themselves weak according to the flesh to see how a man subject to like passions as themselves was so strengthened and used by the Holy Spirit. God chooses weak, frail, and earthen vessels, yea, broken pitchers, to convey His grace. There were times when for a whole week this man was in a very low state, saw only his own backwardness in God's service, and felt only his own indifference to the souls over whom he was set as a watchman. He reproached himself that his thoughts were unduly absorbed with the work in the colony, while all Africa, with its countless millions of pagans, lay untrodden before him, inviting labor. Yet who cannot see that all this dark cloud of self-accusation and reproach was but the smoke beneath which burned the Spirit's divine fires? No one can study the brief record of this seven years' ministry without seeing in this unlettered man one who had in the school of Christ learned the lesson of self-loss for others' gain. He counted himself but a seed of the kingdom, whose destiny it was to die, and dying bring forth much fruit, and that fruit was all the recompense or reward he desired.

What a sign and fruit of God's husbandry was it that in the unpromising soil of Sierra Leone passion for souls was found growing even in new converts! It was common for those who had recently found Christ to be moved by irrepressible desires to win others to Him. For instance, a woman comes, desiring to speak with Mr. Johnson. As Mondays were set apart for spiritual conference and counsel, he bids her come then. But it is midweek, and she cannot wait; her anxieties for others are too intense to brook delay. Yet she herself had been baptized only eight months before, and amid constant persecution from her country-people had persevered both in her piety of conduct and her boldness of testimony. Even her own husband beat her when she talked of Jesus, but she calmly defied his club until his hard heart yielded before her gentle patience, and he began to attend church and sought a habitation nearer by, that he might oftener hear the Word. And now she has brought four of her countrywomen, and they are waiting for the missionary's teaching. Through this humble woman's witness the grace of God has begun in them also its mighty work. Think of a degraded African woman, who eight months before was a fetish-worshiper too low apparently to be reached even by the gospel, and yet whose mighty passion for souls cannot be put off five days for an interview! Where did these debased people get such advanced ideas of divine things, as when another woman of the Ebo tribe came asking for baptism, and said, "Me pray to God the Holy

Ghost to take me to Jesus, Him to take me to the Father"? The pastor could only marvel how to so simple a mind had been revealed the ministry of the Spirit in leading to Jesus as Saviour, and the mediatorial work of the Lord Jesus in reconciling and leading the sinner to God. But the same Spirit who could thus make truth plain to the benighted heart could inspire in that heart a holy zeal for God.

If "the powers that be are ordained of God," they do not always honor their divine ordination. In 1818 the governor, visiting Regent's Town, expressed the wish that Mr. Johnson would baptize more of the people, and, in fact, all of them that would submit. Looking on baptism as he did, as an *act of civilization*, he thought it the duty of the missionary to apply it to all and so help to make them all Christians. He urged that the reason why so many were baptized on the day of Pentecost was that the apostles despised and refused none; and the warmth and positiveness with which he advocated such promiscuous use of the ordinance were well calculated to abash and embarrass his humble subordinate.

Like too many others, the chief magistrate mistook a sign and seal of grace received for a means or method of receiving or conveying grace. Few evils have ever crept into the church of God more alarming and subtle than notions of *sacramental efficacy*. Worship expresses itself in forms, but forms can never inspire worship. Love and loyalty to God find their natural channel in holy obedience, but in vain do you scoop out a channel where there is no stream. It is both an inversion and a perversion when a sacrament or ordinance is elevated to such prominence as that it is made practically to take the position of a cause where it should be an effect, or to precede where it should succeed.

Johnson was not a man to be thus silenced. He could withstand governors and kings if loyalty to Christ and His truth demanded, as John the Baptist rebuked Herod, as Elijah confronted Ahab, or as Sir Matthew Hale joined issue with the Protector. He quietly replied that he could baptize none whose hearts God had not touched.

The simple-minded missionary had clear views of New Testament teaching, and dared to hold firmly fast to apostolic usage, and would baptize no adults save those who, like pentecostal converts, were "pricked in their heart" and "believed." The governor had no answer ready to meet the biblical argument, but had the usual reply, always too easy to resort to, and often quite too convincing to timid souls—the appeal to human authority. He declared he would write to the Archbishop of Canterbury about it, insisting that it was Johnson's duty to *make Christians* of this people. To which again he replied that there was One only who could make Christians, and that he could and would baptize none but those whom he believed God had thus wrought upon. So stubborn was the governor in his purpose to follow out his notions of baptismal regeneration that he threatened to employ some less scrupulous Wesleyan minister to perform the rite, or get more advanced ritualists from the Society for

Promoting Christian Knowledge. Johnson again affirmed his readiness to baptize all who were manifestly penitent for sin and willing to accept Christ as Saviour, but he could not go beyond the Word of the Lord, even at the command of a governor. The chief magistrate gave up the contest as hopeless, and contented himself with calling the immovable Johnson and the society that sent him to Africa "a set of fanatics."

The missionary, who had learned too much of loyalty to God to obey human dictates, found that this was not the only matter in which conscience compelled resistance to the chief magistrate of the colony. He refused to enjoin the people to sing "God save the king," because it was so habitually sung over the beer-pot that he could not safely introduce it into a divine service. And although the governor was determined to impose it on the people, Johnson would not submit, believing this patriotic hymn so tainted with godless associations that it was like a garment spotted with the flesh, unfit to be worn by worshipers in a prayer service.

Whether or not the missionary's course always commends itself to our judgment as wise and sensible, we cannot question either its sincerity or intrepidity; and, in view of the temptation before which so many fail and fall, of bowing to human authority even at expense of conscience, it is impossible not to admire the fixedness of purpose that made him stand like Gibraltar amid the waves, firm, unmoved, and serene.

While in Freetown Christmas was a day of revelry, if not of riot, the people conducting themselves in most unseemly fashion, guns firing all night, drunkenness stalking the streets, houses set on fire, and maroons and settlers ready any moment for an open brawl, Johnson saw in his own field peace and quiet prevailing, a cleanly dressed and decorous company coming to church, without a sound of gun-firing or a sign of intoxication. And the next day eight hundred happy people sat down together to a sort of lovefeast before the house of the missionary. They had themselves prepared the dinner, their carpenters making the tables and benches, and their mechanics bringing the provisions they had saved against the feast-day, while others cooked them. David Noah, one of their number, asked the blessing, which all reverently repeated after him. And when all had eaten and were full, they gathered up the fragments, that nothing might be lost. What a contrast to the cannibal feasts of pagan tribes!

The mighty passion for souls that swayed Johnson had a strong counter-current to contend with in his hearty affection for his wife. In 1819 there first arose a demand, on her account, for a pause in his apostolic work. Mrs. Johnson's health, which during all their stay in Sierra Leone proved very frail, had at this time become seriously and, as it proved, permanently impaired. In 1818 an almost fatal illness had brought her to the verge of the grave, and the same symptoms now reappeared with even greater violence, and made her return to England a matter of necessity. Her devoted husband was in a strait betwixt two, much perplexed as to questions of both love and duty. Loyalty to his wife and responsibility for his large flock each pressed its peculiar claims, and it was for a time doubtful which motive would ultimately prevail. In each direction his path seemed to meet a "mountain insurmountable to reason." At last he determined to accompany her to England.

Here perhaps we come to a natural halting-place whence to look in general survey over the work accomplished in these two short years. As from "Inspiration Point," which in the Yosemite Valley commands a view of the whole of that vale of imposing beauty, we may here at least glance at the stupendous changes wrought by the gospel at Hogbrook.

This repulsive name, which had given place to the more refined title Regent's Town, had come originally from the host of wild hogs which infested the small stream flowing thereabouts; and it was scarce too mean to describe the low order of human swine which were there found wallowing in their own mire and filth. What more could be expected of a refuse population, the offscouring of the earth, swept from the alleys of London, and emptied out of those devil's galleys, the slave-ships, and finding a dumping-ground in Africa! Here in Sierra Leone this indiscriminate mass of humanity, huddled together without moral restraints or physical control, gave way to the basest of animal passions because no higher motives were appealed to; and the life thus lived was so unutterably low in its level, physically, intellectually, and morally, that, as has been intimated, language supplies no proper colors in which to paint such a picture. Hell may furnish an adequate dialect of description, but earth has not yet supplied one, thank God!

Can it be credited, even upon authentic testimony, that already there had taken place a transformation which was rather a transfiguration? Worship simple and sincere, decorous and spiritual, on the Lord's day, family prayer preceding and following daily toils, and such public and household devotions displacing a superstition and idolatry too low to be dignified by the name of worship! Gree-gree charms and witchcraft, red water and devils' houses, vile practices and abhorrent usages, had already given way to decent attire and civilized habits, to Christian wedlock and well-regulated household life, to Bibles and prayer-books, missionary societies and consecrated offerings.

Johnson's passion for souls led to occasional excursions into the surrounding country, a few references to which may be sufficient without repetitious details. For example, early in 1819 he went, in company with Mr. Cates, William Tamba, and others, to Wilberforce, on the northwestern side of the colony, and Cape Shilling, forty miles beyond, to Margenna and Robiss, and made a complete circuit. He undertook tours afoot, going sometimes as far as one hundred and twenty miles in seven days, in hopes to reach those tribes yet unevangelized, and find new fields of service and sacrifice, and win new trophies for Christ. In all these excursions he found it needful almost to tear himself away from the simple-minded converts, who were in mortal fear lest some fatality might take from them the teacher to whom they were devoted. So great, however, was Johnson's yearning to sow the wider wastes about him with the gospel seed that but for providential hindrances arresting his activities he would doubtless have overleaped the bounds of the colony in larger and more permanent operations. He might, indeed, have anticipated Livingstone as Africa's missionary explorer and general.

Everywhere in these tours into regions beyond were found proofs of a similar degradation to that originally confronted in Hogbrook. Among the Cosso people marks of the reign of superstition abounded. Scarce a house had not its wooden post and broken bowl for its defense. At Margenna they were warned against approaching one particular house, as it was haunted, and approach would be fatal; and to confirm this a dead horned owl was pointed out hanging near it, which, as it was stoutly maintained, had dropped down dead for presuming to fly over it.

One important result of this tour (1819) was that both Mr. Johnson and Mr. Cates felt so well satisfied as to the manner in which

William Tamba had addressed the natives that both he and William Davis were taken into the society's service to act as messengers of salvation in native districts. The examination of these two men previous to their being thus set apart revealed the same motives and spirit as in the most mature saints—another evidence of the Spirit's teaching. In their simple language we find a holy humility and self-distrust, coupled with a deep desire to be of use, a simple faith in God's call and help, and a courageous fearlessness in accepting whatever risk was involved. And the society's committee, in approving this new step of sending native teachers among their countrymen, advised a well-digested system whereby competent converts should be selected, trained, and habituated to such evangelistic service.

The secretaries of the Church Missionary Society wrote to Johnson (April 8, 1819), expressing their judgment that he had been "rather too slow to baptize," they taking the position that "baptism is a means of grace, and may be a turning-point in decision of heart for Christ." They also advised that in cases of "baptized persons dying" he might safely "use the burial service, whatever their previous character," arguing that to refuse implied a "needless scrupulosity" and an assuming of "a judgment of condemnation."

The same letter informed him that a second chaplain, the Rev. Thomas Garnsey, was about to come to the colony.

While the critical illness of Mrs. Johnson made her immediate return to England necessary, and demanded his accompanying her (for she needed such care as only a husband can give), yet it seemed impossible to leave the people. Over fifty negroes were added in February to the church, and many more were candidates, so that nearly every night was spent in examination; and some cases of conversion were as startling as the change of a lion into a lamb.

As the time drew near for Mr. Johnson to sail for England the need seemed to be only the more imperative for him to remain where he was. The number of communicants now reached two hundred and sixty-three, and their course of life was such as became the gospel of Christ, and put to silence all caviling. All the people seemed hungry for righteousness, and a deep seriousness pervaded the schools. Moreover, in March, 1819, the boys' school-house was burned, and the girls' house and Johnson's own dwelling were in danger; but prayer was earnestly offered for deliverance, and the wind, which at the beginning was so boisterous as to threaten a conflagration, ceased, and a complete calm followed, and all the people saw the *flames ascend perpendicularly*, and acknowledged the hand of God. Such destruction made necessary a rebuilding, while such interposition of God emphasized the power of prayer and opened the hearts of the people to the truth. On April 11, 1819, Mr. Johnson baptized one hundred and ten adults; it was a pentecostal day.

The missionary who saw this work of God moving at such pace in Regent's Town not only went on evangelistic tours into the regions beyond, but sought to organize missionary societies and multiply all kindred means of gracious growth and service in the settlements he visited. Though at times very low-spirited, he found refuge from morbid mental states in abundant work for others, and when so ill that he seemed pressed down under an insupportable burden of discouragement, he remembered that we are "immortal till our work is done," and gloried in that strength which is made perfect only in weakness.

These venturings into the regions beyond were sometimes occasions of peculiar interest. During the nine days' journey in October, 1820, in connection with the Plantains,—a group of islands where he found about two hundred inhabitants,—Mr. Johnson went in search of the lime-trees planted by the Rev. John Newton when he had been wandering over the island like a lost sheep; and he found that they had been cut down, but from the trunk of one new branches had shot forth; and a hymn-book also was discovered, several hymns in which were of Newton's own composition. Thus, on the very spot where this converted slave-trader had wandered in ignorance sixty-five years before, and planted lime-trees for his amusement, his hymns were still being sung in the Sherbro tongue.

In April, 1821, Johnson learned that the missionaries had succeeded in getting land sufficient to begin a colony in the Bassa country. When the news reached his ears his emotion could not be expressed. Mr. Cates had been encouraged to go into that country with reference to establishing a mission, and he had died of fatigue, which had caused Johnson to bear a heavy burden. Now, for the first time, that burden had been relieved, for had Mr. Cates not gone there, the missionaries would not have received land. The king had made an agreement with him which opened the way immediately, and now the prince, the king's son, came with Mr. Davis as a token of good faith. When the two entered the evening school, the natives of the Bassa country surrounded the prince, affectionately embraced him, and inquired for their relatives, laughing for joy when they heard that their parents were alive and that the gospel would soon be sounding in their ears. The scene was simply indescribable, and would have drawn tears from eyes unused to weep.

There was a sense in which the regions beyond were frequently brought near to the missionary's doors. On May 15, 1821, a note received from J. Reffell, Esq., chief superintendent of captured negroes, informed Johnson that a vessel had been brought in with two hundred and thirty-eight miserable slaves, and that he and the acting governor had agreed to send them up to Regent's Town, begging him to go to Freetown to receive them. He went, accompanied by some of the people, those who remained at home preparing food for these new-comers. The vessel was a small schooner, and many of the poor victims were actually reduced to skeletons. Two hundred and seventeen slaves were delivered to Johnson's care, the rest being placed in the Leicester Hospital. He had to surround them by his people as they marched out of Freetown to prevent the soldiers of the fort seizing some of the women for wives.

The scenes which took place upon the arrival of these slaves at Regent's Town defy description. As soon as they came in sight all the people left their houses to meet them with loud acclamations. When they saw that the new-comers were weak and faint, they carried the feeblest of them toward Mr. Johnson's house and laid them on the ground, themselves also being quite exhausted. Soon many of the people began to recognize their friends and relatives, and there was a general cry: "O massa, my sister, my brother, my mother, my father, my countrywoman!" The poor creatures, who had recently been taken out of the hold of a slave-vessel, faint and but half conscious of what had befallen them, did not know whether to laugh or cry when they beheld the countenances of those whom they had supposed long dead, but whom they now beheld, clothed and clean, in some cases perhaps bearing healthy children in their arms. The people ran off to their houses, brought all the provisions they had made ready, and shortly overpowered these unfortunates with messes of every description, pineapples, oranges, and groundnuts being also brought out in great abundance.

During the same day another remarkable event occurred—nothing less than a genuine earthquake, which shook all the buildings; but even this made less impression than the wonderful scenes of the morning, and it was a long time before these lost their vividness.

These new-comers had to be distributed among the people, several of whom had the joy to take home a long-lost brother or sister. There were many most affecting incidents. One of the little girls who had been rescued was clothed in the raiment of a school-girl, that she might be taken to church; and when she saw the number of people gathered, she ran back crying, thinking it was a slave-market and she was again to be sold. She stammered out among sobs that she "had been sold too much, and did not want to be sold any more." By October fifty out of two hundred and thirty-eight of the newly arrived slaves had died as the effect of their confinement and half-starvation on shipboard.

Another addition had now to be planned for the church, which was enlarged so as to be eighty feet long by sixty-four wide, with galleries all around, doubling its accommodations.

Notwithstanding his trials, labors, and disappointments, Johnson felt himself to be the happiest man in the world, and declared that he would not exchange his situation for all the crowns on earth; while, at the same time, he was so affected by the sins and waywardness of the people that he was a Jeremiah, and exclaimed, "Oh that my head were waters, and mine eyes a fountain of tears, that I might weep day and night for the slain of the daughter of my people!" In October, 1822, one hundred and eighty more were received from a slave-vessel, thus increasing the population to nineteen hundred. The regions beyond were sending their population to his very doors.

CHAPTER VIII

IN THE FURNACE OF AFFLICTION

THE spirit is often willing when the flesh is weak. It is one of the sore trials of faith that in more senses than one it has to wrestle against flesh and blood. Weakness hinders even those who are no longer slaves of wickedness, and infirmities of the body oppress many a saint who is strong in faith and heroic in purpose. To learn to halt for a time, especially for an indefinite time, and, while yearning and burning with intense desire for active service, to be compelled to rest, perhaps to resign ourselves to passive suffering—this is one of the last and hardest tasks given us in the school of God.

In Johnson's case such an abandonment of his work first became a necessity in 1819. He had long fought against it, but at last succumbed to an inevitable, unavoidable absence, and knew not when he would return. A mysterious divine hand pointed to the shores of Britain a man whose whole heart, like Livingstone's after him, was in Africa.

The day of departure came, and on April 22d—a farewell message to his beloved people, from 2 Corinthians xiii. 11 having been delivered four days previously—Johnson embarked on board the *Echo*. Hundreds of negroes, old and young, men and women, walked with him over the hard five-mile road to Freetown, and took leave of him with many tears, as the Ephesian elders parted from Paul at Miletus. They gave striking expression to their devotion in such simple words as these: "Massa, suppose no water live here," pointing to the wide sea, "we go with you all the way *till feet no more.*"

Such a man as Johnson could not be hid. On the voyage he preached, and dealt so faithfully and pointedly with the passengers that some complained to the captain that the preacher was personal. It was the message, not the man, that was "personal"; and so plain was it that he was impelled only by unselfish love of truth and love of souls that before the vessel reached the dock the mouths of opposers were stopped, and foes were turned to friends, kind and attentive.

As the main purpose of this narrative is to portray with all possible simplicity and brevity the work of God at Sierra Leone, it will suffice to give only a passing glance at this interval of absence from the field.

He revisited Hanover in Germany, where his mother lived, and when he told her that he was her son, her own "Augustine," she could not believe it until he showed her two marks upon his body which served to identify him. Then her agitation of mind can scarcely be conceived. Tears of mingled joy and uncontrollable excitement ran down her cheeks. One of his sisters, about twenty years old, could not be persuaded to leave him, and scarcely slept after his arrival, sitting beside him even when he lay in bed. Notwithstanding his own disapproval of the plan as inexpedient, she prepared to accompany him wherever he might go, and, following him on his return to England, she was, after due examination, received by the committee of the Church Missionary Society as a schoolmistress for West Africa. Thus Johnson's visit to his own kindred was attended with peculiar blessing, for which his gracious experiences and letters had prepared the way, and lasting impressions were made upon a large circle of relatives and friends.

While in England, God used his simple narrative of his missionary labors in Sierra Leone, as he had used the rehearsal of the mission tour of Paul and Barnabas at Antioch, for the refreshment and arousing of the churches. The respite from work at Regent's Town was not a loss to the wider work of missions. For example, when, before the Berkshire Church Missionary Association, he read letters lately received from native converts and communicants in his church in Sierra Leone,—Tamba, Davis, Peter Hughes, David Noah,—a gentleman who was present was so struck with these letters as confirming Mr. Johnson's statements that he asked to be informed whether these documents were originals or copies. He was permitted to examine them closely for himself, and he then frankly stated his conviction that, considering the very short time during which these slaves had been under instruction, they evinced a degree and a rapidity of progress in religious knowledge quite unequaled.* He was so persuaded of the usefulness of Mr. Johnson's labors that, although a member and supporter both of the Society for Promoting Christian Knowledge and of the Society for the Propagation of the Gospel in Foreign Parts, he could not withhold active support from the Church Missionary Society also, and it was at his suggestion that a resolution was passed favoring the publication of these letters. Mr. Johnson attended meetings and addressed audiences at Saffron-Walden, Suffolk, Exeter, Teignmouth, and other places, and everywhere great blessing attended his words of witness. But Sierra Leone drew him with a strange and irresistible force, and, as Mrs. Johnson's health was already greatly improved, in less than five months after his

* Appendix II.

arrival in England preparations were made for his return. On the 19th of November, at Freemasons' Hall in London, he gave a detailed account of the remarkable scenes of transformation he had already witnessed at Regent's Town, and it is difficult to say which produced the profounder impression—the marvelous changes of which he had been the instrumental means, or the simplicity and humility which were manifested in the whole narration. The minds of all present were deeply moved, and this brief visit to England served to rivet attention upon the field to which he returned.

On December 27th, with their band of new helpers, he and his wife reëmbarked for Africa in the ship *Maida*, and on January 31, 1820, reached Freetown.

On landing he was met, as might be anticipated, by a welcome home which was characteristically hearty. A man who saw him coming ashore ran quickly five miles to Regent's Town with the news; and Mr. Wilhelm had just concluded the daily evening service when he rushed in among the congregation crying, "All hear! all hear! Mr. Johnson come!" The confusion and excitement overleaped all bounds. The whole assembly leaped to its feet as one man, and such as could not wait to get out at the doors actually jumped out at the windows. Mr. Johnson testified that he had never in his life shaken hands as on that day, though he took care not to *lose any of his finger-nails* in consequence of this incessant and painful handshaking, as had been the case when he left six months before. But the joy of those simple-minded people made him quite insensible to any physical discomfort due to their wild enthusiasm.

One of the first matters claiming his attention was a letter which had come, in his absence, from the secretaries in London, having reference to the loud outcries and violent fits of weeping, already noted as often hindering the decorous conduct of public worship. The letter called attention to the necessity of carefully guarding against Satan's devices, and referred to the peculiar character of the African tribes, their imperfect knowledge of religion and their limited experience in the divine life, their imperfectly formed judgments and their constitutional susceptibility to excitement. The wisdom of a sound mind, evinced in this whole communication, showed that the Church Missionary Society then, as now, was administered by men conspicuous not only for sterling piety, but for sanctified common sense. Johnson felt, however, what many a missionary has felt since, that it is one thing to give wise counsel from a secretary's desk in the center of an enlightened nation, and quite another to confront an actual difficulty on the field, in the midst of an ignorant, uncultivated, superstitious throng of negroes recently rescued from the yoke of abject slavery. Many a theory of treatment, which is as symmetrical and beautiful as the geometrical web which a spider weaves, is as frail and weak when applied to the practical evil which needs correction or restraint. It reminds one of the boastful French surgeon who, having treated a large number of critical cases, confessed that he had in no case saved the patient's life, but insisted that *the operation was very brilliant.*

A supreme sorrow and trial, however,

awaited Mr. Johnson's return. When he entered Regent's Town it was about ten o'clock in the evening and bright moonlight; but that silver radiance only served to disclose the fact that ruins confronted him everywhere. The church tower and the school-house, which was being roofed in when he left, were now leveled to the ground; the other school-house, intended for the boys, was pulled down as far as the windows, and the fences were down about his yard and garden and the cultivated field. The hospital was as he had left it, no progress having been made, and all else, including the church building, was in a most deplorable state. In fact, the town was scarcely recognizable.

Closer examination showed more serious declension in spiritual things. Several of his church-members had sadly backslidden, but not without cause. In his subsequent letter to the directors he says: "I thought that I had left a friend and a brother here when I left this place,* but how have I been deceived!" Rachel Garnon, Hagar Johnson,

* By his own request a Mr. and Mrs. Morgan had been put in charge of the work during his absence.

and Martha Johnson had actually been flogged out of church, on Sunday, by his substitute. These girls had for three years been Mr. Johnson's household servants, and one of them had just risen from a sick-bed. Rachel bore for considerable time the marks of the whip on her back; nor could the victims of this outrage tell why this flogging had been inflicted, or why they were thus driven from the house of worship. Mrs. Wilhelm gave them all an excellent character, attesting their uniformly consistent Christian behavior.

It gradually transpired that, so soon as Johnson had gone, his plans had been upset and new ones formed, and the whole town brought into confusion. The pay of some of the work-people had been reduced, and such as were not willing to accept less wages had been told to go elsewhere, so that the population of the place had, from this and other causes, been thinned. The missionary society had been virtually dissolved; no one had for four or five months spoken of it or done anything to feed its flame, no sermon being preached, no offerings being collected; and a fire that has no fuel will of course die down and go out. The benefit society would likewise have gone to ruin had not the members of it themselves kept up the interest in it.

Mr. Wilhelm had done all he could to restore former prosperity, but with only partial success. Through an administration so unwise as to be almost, if not quite, unchristian, the little church had been well-nigh wrecked. Yet all that Mr. Johnson wrote to the directors was without a trace of resentment: "I pity Mr. ——, and heartily forgive him, and pray that, if he goes out again elsewhere, he may be possessed of a more humble spirit."

With the return of the beloved pastor the church rapidly regained its former state. He invited and exhorted the people to come together, revive their missionary society and renew their offerings, and they cordially responded. The church had gone through the furnace of trial and was not consumed; over two hundred and fifty communicants remained, and on this basis the rebuilding of the work must be carried on.

As in every other crisis, God's servant resorted to prayer. As he confronted the disasters that in his absence had come upon the little flock, under a grief that would have crushed most other men, he simply took refuge in the old promise through which the light first came into his soul:

> "Call upon Me in the day of trouble;
> I will deliver thee, and thou shalt glorify Me."

A prayer-hearing God once more appeared for his deliverance. At the throne of grace in the secret pavilion with God he got peace and so communicated it, removing the jealousy and envy which had been the cause of all the differences between brethren, and himself setting the example of unselfish love. He himself never caused unpleasantness or estrangement. Bearing patiently with a meek and quiet spirit all that was unkind and unjust, he became not only a peacekeeper, but a peacemaker, though never at the expense of truth or the risk of principles. "The wisdom that is from above is *first* pure, then peaceable."

His holy zeal was, throughout, a large factor

in his success. In the midst of all these arduous toils, made heavier by these trials, he writes: "Ah, who would not be a missionary to Africa! Had I ten thousand lives, I would willingly offer them all for the sake of one poor negro." Such devotion is the impregnable armor of love, and enables one to bear all things and be more than a conqueror.

His humility also made him self-distrustful and therefore the less prone to judge others harshly. He did not wince under reproof, but rather sought rebuke when needful. He begged the secretaries to counsel and admonish him as to whatever they regarded as out of the way; he thought of himself as a most unworthy and inefficient missionary, and welcomed even a smiting as a kindness if it might help him to greater service.

No small part of the distressing vexations of this field arose from resident Europeans, as, for example, those in Freetown, whose ungodly passions found vent not only in breaking the Sabbath for themselves, but in getting intoxicated and going about on horseback through the villages, annoying church-goers who were on their way to or from the house of worship.

One of the native converts expressed his quaint philosophy of the trials through which they had passed in these words: "Suppose somebody beat rice; he fan it, and all the chaff fly away and the rice get clean. Now, massa, we be in that fashion since you gone: God fan us that time for true."

In January, 1821, in a letter to the secretaries in London, Johnson made mention of another trial which it was for him very hard patiently to bear, as it involved risk to the converts, over whom he watched with parental care and to whom he was daily imparting his own life and soul, because they were so dear to him. Let us record his own words:

"The devil," he writes, "is going about in two different shapes—like a roaring lion, and like an angel of mercy. Some of our people have become very wicked, and communicants suffer persecution; but this only shows the difference between the seed of the woman and the seed of the serpent. Thirty men and women are under instruction with reference to baptism."

Two months later a severe cold settled upon his lungs, inducing violent coughing and nearly proving fatal. This added greatly to his burdens. About the same time a spirit of opposition and persecution seemed to be let loose among the people. Mere professors of religion, who had no real hold upon the truth or upon the Lord Jesus, carried to and fro by every wind of doctrine and made the victims of the sleight and cunning craftiness of deceivers, joined the openly profane and spoke against him and his co-workers in scorn and ridicule. He felt like David when pursued by enemies who lay in wait for him on every side; but, like David, he found a strong tower of refuge in God, and the work of Christ proceeded.

There was another fire of trial through which Johnson was called to pass; in fact, it might be said that he was never out of this furnace of affliction, though its heat was not always equally intense. We refer to his overwhelming conviction of his own sinfulness and unworthiness. He was a marvelous missionary in the measure of his simple faith, implicit obedience, and successful work. Yet the more God's mercy and goodness were displayed to him, the more unworthy and ungrateful he seemed to himself to be. The goodness of God in a very emphatic sense led him to repentance. It appeared to him as though no human creature could be more depraved, and he records his conviction that in the whole world of sinners there could be no one worse than himself. How far these were morbid moods, owing in part to constitutional habits of self-reproach and in part to diseased conditions of body, it is now impossible to determine. But of one thing no doubt is left: he had learned the great lesson that the only ground of hope which is at all solid and unchanging is that which is external, not internal—a salvation which is of free and saving grace and quite independent of all human merit; and, like Matthew Henry, if he had not at all times the faith of assurance, he had the faith of adherence, and never was left to despair.

Few sorrows cut so deeply as those which are vicarious, and most of all when evil threatens our best beloved. "A sword shall pierce thine own soul also," was the brief but awful forecast of the anguish which the virgin mother of our Lord would suffer when the spear should pierce His human heart. Mrs. Johnson's illness in 1822 was so severe that the doctors directed her immediate departure for Europe; an ulcer was forming in her head; and on the 4th of May she took leave of her husband. The people mourned her departure, declaring that she was to them "like their own mother," which was true. They were prostrated by grief, and every one appeared to mourn and weep. Johnson felt that he must not again leave his people, for he could not forget how, when the shepherd had before parted with his flock for a season, the wolf had been among them and had caught some and scattered the whole flock. Yet he endured a great fight of contending feelings.

When, five months after Mrs. Johnson had thus sailed for England alone, a rumor was spread by an arriving vessel that she had died at sea, her husband's mind was kept for months in most painful suspense, more especially as another vessel, that left England a month after the arrival of the *Fletcher*, brought no letter from Mr. Düring and no tidings from Mrs. Johnson. And yet, in the midst of all these labors and anxieties, he redoubled his activities, if that were possible, and enjoyed unusual power and freedom in preaching. From every new distraction of care he found escape in absorbing work for God and souls, and the promise was again fulfilled: "As thy days so shall thy strength be." Sometimes for five hours he spoke, yet without undue fatigue; and although again the church building had been enlarged, the audiences were too great to be accommodated.

The report of Mrs. Johnson's death was not confirmed, as on November 21st a letter from the captain of the *Fletcher* to a gentleman in Freetown stated that all his passengers had been safely landed. It subsequently transpired, however, that Mr. Johnson's mother was dead, and the surviving members of the household at home were in consequence plunged into the depths of sorrow.

Africa was indeed a "vale of tears," and Mr. Johnson's own testimony was, "If any one wishes to experience trials, let him come to Africa. It is certainly the worst climate in the world." And yet so much was this man inspired by passion for souls, and so deeply was he interested in his work and his people, that he adds, "There is nevertheless not a spot in the world that I like better. I could not live elsewhere." How like David Livingstone that sounds! He was in the furnace of affliction in Africa for thirty years. Yet nothing could wean him from his love for the Dark Continent.

CHAPTER IX

THE CLOUD OF WITNESSES

Of all the forms of the self-life, none is more subtle than self-glory. Many a servant of God has been so lifted up with pride by his own successes as to be utterly disqualified for further use. And so the severest test of a true workman is this: whether, amid all the highest honor given him of God in service, he not only retains humility, but grows in this consummate grace, which Andrew Murray regards as the very "beauty of holiness."

"Let another praise thee, and not thine own mouth," is a maxim that seldom needs to be repeated to a true servant of God, for he well knows that all glory belongs to his Master, since all power is from Him. The mouth that is active in one's own praise is the sad index of a heart that has not learned that primal secret of all service, that, even when labors are most abundant and harvests most plentiful, both the strength for the toil and the increase from the seed-sowing are the bestowments of God.

Johnson never glorified himself; and, in fact, he saw nothing in himself to awaken complacency or afford ground for boasting, so that his humility rather grew as his success increased. Consequently the major part of this great work of God would never have been thus widely known had not a cloud of witnesses, not only from within but from without the mission, been constrained to bear testimony.

At this distance of time it is difficult to appreciate the rapidity with which the transformation of the community at Regent's Town went forward. Mr. Renner, the senior missionary in western Africa, after a visit thus wrote, as early as January 2, 1817, to Mr. Pratt, of the Church Missionary Society: "I spoke morning and evening in the church to a people that seemed to be devout indeed. Regent's Town is fast advancing in getting civilized and Christianized. Almost every night, as I am told, one or another is affected, and on certain nights the whole congregation seem impressed. Judging by appearance, these are they that take the kingdom of heaven by violence. The temporal and spiritual work of our brother is no doubt great and laborious among this people, but to Johnson all is easy and full of pleasure. It is surprising to what a degree of harmonious singing both sexes have attained, as if it were a congregation of ten years' standing."

Sunday, November 23, 1817, Captain Welsh of the brig *Pyrenees* spent at Regent's Town, having been an old acquaintance of Johnson's in London. When the bell rang the first time, Johnson and Welsh themselves found it difficult, and in fact impossible, to get in by the doors, and had to find their way through the church tower. Not only was the building thus filled, but some were sitting outside on boards. The sermon was from John v. 6: "Wilt thou be made whole?" Captain Welsh was delighted, and said, "I have to-day seen what I never saw before. What would not our London friends give for such a sight! God has blessed your labors beyond description. I had heard of your success, but could not believe what I heard." The modest missionary could only reply, as usual: "To God be all the glory," for he habitually turned attention from himself to Him who is the fountain of all blessing.

Mr. Morgan—who had undertaken the administration of the mission during Mr. Johnson's absence, and who had exhibited, as we have seen, such surprising lack of good temper, administrative skill, and Christian discretion, if nothing worse, and who was entirely recalled from the field in consequence—would not be very likely to give any too partial an account of Johnson's work. Yet on his return to London he made to the committee a report which has the highest value, because it cannot have been colored by any personal attachment to his predecessor, from whom he had in some measure been alienated. Such testimony borne to another's success is a proof of its reality which cannot be set aside, and should be embodied in this narrative.*

When Æschines heard unstinted praise of Demosthenes' oration "On the Crown," he was constrained to say, notwithstanding that oration was directed against himself, "Ah, you should have heard it yourself; it was a masterpiece!" And what shall we say when even the verdict of foes also was in Johnson's favor? When Satan bestirs himself against God's servants, it is probably because his craft is in danger. It was when Paul and his fellow-witnesses were turning the Ephesian world upside down that Demetrius raised his uproar. In 1821 a West Indian rumseller—whose infernal business was fast coming to ruin through the faithful preaching of Johnson against drunkenness and all that led to it—lay in wait with a loaded gun to shoot him; and so obvious was his murderous intent that, after repeated proofs had been afforded of his hateful malice, the missionary unwillingly lodged a complaint against him. But that man's loaded gun was

* Appendix III.

an indirect witness to the work of reformation. Satan may well war against a transformation so radical that it was rather a transfiguration.

In the report of the local authorities at Sierra Leone sent to the home government in January, 1819, such changes as have been described were formally noted, and the official document thus concludes (let us embody the very words, as a most emphatic testimony on the part of secular magistrates):

"Let it be considered that not more than three or four years have passed since the greater number of Mr. Johnson's population were taken out of the holds of slaveships; and who can compare their present condition with that from which they were rescued without seeing manifest cause to exclaim, 'The hand of Heaven is in this'! Who can contrast the simple and sincere Christian worship which precedes and follows their daily labors with the groveling and malignant superstitions of their original state —their gree-grees, their red water, their witchcraft, and their devils' houses—without feeling and acknowledging a miracle of good which the immediate interposition of the Almighty alone could have wrought? And what greater blessing could man or nation desire or enjoy than to have been made the instruments of conferring such sublime benefits on the most abject of the human race?

"If any other circumstance could be required to prove the immediate interposition of the Almighty, we have only to look at the plain men and simple means employed in bringing about the miraculous conversion that we have recorded. Does it not recall to mind the first diffusion of the gospel by the apostles themselves? These thoughts will occur to strangers at remote distance when they hear these things, and must they not recur much more forcibly to us who have these things constantly before our eyes?"

Another notable testimony was given in April, 1819, by Mr. and Mrs. Jesty, who, having just come to reinforce the missionary band, paid a visit to the field, and bore their witness. Mrs. Jesty wrote to her sister:

"I wish that I could find language sufficiently descriptive of the interesting scenes which we have witnessed here. Indeed, they must be seen before the facts will be credited. Had I heard the circumstances from the best authority, I could not have conceived it possible that so glorious a progress could have been made in the work of our God as we have beheld since we have been staying at Regent's Town." *

In April, 1821, Mr. Singleton, a member of the Society of Friends, sent out to glean facts about the Dark Continent, arrived at Regent's Town, and was so deeply moved by what he saw that he was scarcely able to speak. He was astonished to see these wretched slaves now so clean and tidy, their general condition so much better than that of the poorer classes in Great Britain; and to find Bibles and Testaments everywhere on the tables in their houses as familiar books.

A humorous incident occurred in connection with Mr. Singleton's visit. Quaker-like, he entered the church without taking off his hat. This was an act quite inexplicable to

* Appendix IV.

the native Christians, and seemed to them shockingly irreverent; so that two of them boldly went up to him and politely requested him to remove his hat, which he did with a smile, apparently much pleased with their zeal for God, although in a sense it was not according to knowledge. At the evening meeting he heard from one of the native women a very pathetic and effective testimony:

"When me think about the great things God has done for me, me do not know what to do. When me was in my own country they catch us all, and then they take up my brothers and sisters and kill them. Me only left,"— here her sobs almost choked her utterance,— "and they put them in the pot and boil them and eat them. Me only left. What great things the Lord do for me! Poor, guilty sinner, me so bad! Only the good Lord Jesus save me."

On Mr. Singleton's return he published a journal of his tour and a report, in which he refers to Regent's Town and the great work of God there.*

It was during this same year, 1821, that the

* Appendix V.

Europeans of Freetown, after an inspection, confessed their surprise at the order, industry, and piety of the people, and were especially amazed at their liberality, they having that year contributed over seventy-two pounds sterling (three hundred and fifty dollars). The mouths of opposers and critics were so effectually stopped that they acknowledged the gospel to be the only adequate means of civilizing such heathen; and the gentlemen of Freetown were so thoroughly convinced of the general success of preaching the gospel that they publicly paid their tribute that, above all other institutions, those of Regent's Town had proved most beneficial to the degraded children of ‿Africa. Editors sought interviews with reference to publishing accounts of the work, and, what is a more crucial test, many of these European residents, and among them the governor, *asked Johnson to call upon them for contributions!* In fact, this humble man was in fear lest the prosperity that exposed him to so much flattery might involve serious risk of inflating him with pride.

An American vessel arrived in March, 1821,

with missionaries for the Sherbro coast. Two of them, Messrs. Andrus and Bacon, visited the church at Regent's Town. Mr. Andrus left on record his testimony that he had supposed the accounts which he had heard to be greatly exaggerated, but, like the Queen of Sheba, he felt that the half had not been told him. He had never, even in America, seen any church filled with more devout and decorous hearers, nor so large a body of communicants behaving with more piety at the Lord's table. Mr. Bacon, the other of these American visitors, on his return to Philadelphia published a glowing account of his experiences in Africa, which we likewise preserve as essential to the completeness of this volume.*

We record another unequivocal tribute to this work of God through His servant. In 1822, at a quarter-session at Freetown, his honor the chief justice observed that "ten years before, when the population of the colony was but four thousand, there were forty cases on the calendar for trial; but that

* Appendix VI.

now, with a population of sixteen thousand, there were but six cases," and he congratulated the magistrates on the moral improvement of the colony. What was most noticeable, however, was the fact that, among the criminal cases, there was not *one* from any of the villages under the superintendence of a missionary or schoolmaster; so that his honor dismissed Johnson and his constables politely, as having no business that required their attendance at the session. The community at Regent's Town represented a law-abiding and self-governing, as well as self-supporting and self-propagating, church. On December 27, 1821, at a meeting of communicants, a law had been framed by themselves, that if any person should begin a quarrel or behave as did not become a Christian, he should be turned out and fined five pounds, or be confined in the house of correction for two months. All, however, conducted themselves with such propriety that there was found no need to put this law into execution.

The work was its own witness. Many a lion was turned into a lamb, and inquiring souls who, like Noah's dove, could find no rest, sought refuge in the ark of the covenant. Johnson's methods with candidates were very thorough. When he received them for instruction he appointed a time when all should be present; he then read over their names, places of abode, etc., and requested certain communicants to watch over them, and if they should observe in them any improper conduct to inform him; and in all cases of unbecoming behavior the offender was dismissed or kept on a sort of probation. All candidates were kept three months on trial, subject to a searching scrutiny. This was found to be the most efficient method of getting acquainted with the real conduct and character of intending communicants. No pains were spared to put to proof the reality of conversion.

Few forms of witness are more convincing and irresistible than those found in the death of saints. The august exchange of worlds is a crisis in any man's history, and in most cases a decisive test of genuineness and sincerity. A faith and hope and love that, in the darkness of the dying hour, light up the valley of the shadow of death with the celestial torch of a confident assurance may well be the object of the envy of the unbeliever; and Balaam is not the only slave of greed or other unholy appetites and passions who has inwardly said, "Let me die the death of the righteous, and let my last end be like his."

Johnson saw converted slaves not only living, but dying, in the full assurance of their high calling. For example, on Easter Sunday, 1820, he was called to attend the funeral of a youth by the name of George Paull, and spoke from Hebrews ix. 27: "It is appointed unto men once to die, but after this the judgment." Concerning the dead, he sent home a tribute whose main outline features we here preserve.

Five years previous to his death he had been taken from the hold of a slave-ship a mere lad. In 1817 he came begging to be taken into the school, and was admitted, and within a year he showed signs of unusual seriousness and sobriety of mind, and shortly gave such evidence of the working of God's grace that he was welcomed into the church and baptized on Christmas day, 1818. From that time his walk with God was obvious to all observers. Habitually earnest and fervent in spirit, he exhibited singular power in prayer and skill in winning souls. A severe cold, caught during the rainy season of 1819, fixed itself upon him and brought on a fatal attack of lung disease. When he died he had already about him the distinguishing marks of a mature and experienced saint. His counsels were wise, his rebukes tender; his expressions of faith in God and resignation to His will most Christ-like; his joy in God and his heavenly insight into truth such as are seen in connection only with the ripest fruits of godliness; and all these characteristics seemed incredible in a lad of sixteen. The slave-boy had in a very peculiar sense been made into the Lord's freeman, and knew not only the clean heart, but the right, the holy, the free spirit. He had thus early learned both the joy of God's salvation and the secret of converting sinners unto God.*

Toward the close of the year 1820 the anni-

* Ps. li. 12, 13.

versary of the Sierra Leone Church Missionary Society was observed. Twenty-one missionaries in all sat down at the same board, the largest number that had ever dined together in the western African mission field. Out of the whole income of the society Mr. Johnson's humble church had that year contributed nearly one half, considerably over fifty pounds sterling.

Thus, from a multitude of independent sources came one consenting testimony to the work of God's grace at Regent's Town.

CHAPTER X

AT THE DESIRED HAVEN

To everything earthly there cometh the end, but to the true saint and servant of God that end is but the beginning of something nobler, better, purer, and more satisfying. Life here ends, that life elsewhere may begin; or rather let us say of the disciple's life that at death it is left free to find its fullest exercise, development, and enjoyment.

In no one thing, perhaps, does our current unbelief more reveal itself than in our cemeteries, where over the graves of our sainted dead we rear monuments with essentially heathen emblems and symbols. What place have inverted torches, closed urns, broken columns, fading flowers, in resting-places of saints? If to be absent from the body is to be present with the Lord, these symbols of disaster, defeat, disappointment, destruction, are wholly unfit to express our faith and hope. Our blessed Lord taught the skeptical Sadducees that God is not the God of the dead, but of the living, and that those whom we call dead all live unto Him. And the Spirit speaketh expressly of the blessedness of the dead who die in the Lord, that, though they rest from their *labors,*—vexatious toils, burdensome exertions,—their *works*—their truest activities—accompany them into the higher sphere; and that they are before the throne of God and serve Him day and night in His temple. And the last glimpse we get of them in the Apocalypse, where the door is opened in heaven, is that of a sevenfold perfection, where there is:

1. "No more curse"—perfect sinlessness;
2. "The throne of God and of the Lamb" —perfect government;
3. "And His servants shall serve Him"— perfect service;
4. "And they shall see His face"—perfect communion;

5. "And His name shall be in their foreheads"—perfect resemblance;

6. "No night there"—perfect day;

7. "And they shall reign for ever and ever"—perfect glory.

Johnson's earthly work was now almost done. In seven years he had effected results which would ordinarily be regarded as an abundant reward, if crowning the labor of a full lifetime. But all this extensity and intensity of holy toils had told upon his physical frame and spirits. Though not yet forty years old, his zeal had been self-consuming, and his health was steadily and rapidly declining. At this time Mrs. Johnson was so much better that hope was entertained of her being able soon to return to Africa; but the last attack of ophthalmia had so seriously impaired the sight of her husband's left eye, and sympathetically of the right eye also, as to threaten him with blindness; and he had been so frequently scorched in the furnace of African fever that his whole constitution was undermined. In February, 1823, he made his last report to the secretaries of the Church Missionary Society, and through it we may get our last survey of the work before he left it forever.

There were then ten different stations in Sierra Leone, with an aggregate of 603 communicants, 410 of whom were at Regent's Town; and of the total number of scholars (3168) 933 were under his care. In this letter he refers to the qualifications of missionaries and schoolmasters needed at Sierra Leone, recommending that they be acquainted not only with the gospel, but with husbandry and mechanics, arithmetic, geography, and land-surveying, and that, withal, they should know how to rule well their own houses. This shows the sagacity of this missionary statesman, who, with all his humble estimate of his own capacity, had set before him this aim: to rear on African soil a *Metlakahtla*—a model state—out of the refuse of humanity that he found at Hogbrook.

At this time he was ministering to the largest congregation he had ever seen gathered in Africa, and the church building, with all its repeated enlargements, was far too small.

Communicants were sometimes obliged to remain outside, especially when for any reason converts from other stations met with those at Regent's Town; and yet the edifice would accommodate two thousand, and he was perplexed how to provide for any more.

The schools were improving, and over seven hundred had been taught to read. The converts, poor as they were, were systematic, habitual, self-denying givers, and a single offering, taken at the meeting of the Regent's Town Branch Missionary Association, amounted to over ten pounds (fifty dollars.)

These are a few only of the indications of the abundant prosperity of the work of God at this stage of its history. It seemed nevertheless so imperative, on the whole, that Johnson should at least rest for a season, that the secretaries agreed to his return to England, and toward the end of April he embarked. When he set sail for England, the superintendence of Regent's Town devolved upon Mr. Norman.

His journal makes mention of one Sarah Bickersteth, the first of her nation who had tasted that the Lord is gracious. She was a native of the Kroo country, and some five years previously, while yet a little girl, had been brought to the colony. She was now well grown, and, being a thoroughly new creature, was very sad over the superstitions of her country people, and very desirous to serve her newly found Saviour in missionary labors. This young woman was Johnson's companion on the voyage, and to her care was committed also an infant daughter of Mr. and Mrs. Düring.

It was but the third day of the voyage when the seeds of the fatal disease which Johnson must have carried on board with him began to manifest their fruits. He was prostrated by a fever, which so increased in intensity and violence that two days later he was too weak even to turn in bed, and his general symptoms were such that, anticipating the end as near at hand, he said to his weeping attendant, "I think I cannot live." On Saturday, the 3d of May, he expressed a deep desire to see his wife once more, and sought to calm the fears of Sarah Bickersteth, who could not calmly contemplate his approaching departure, and he composedly directed her how to proceed on her arrival at London. At his request she then read to him the same Twenty-third Psalm which to so many saints in the valley of the shadow of death has been God's staff and stay; and then adding, "I am dying; pray for me," he passed into the haven where he desired to be. Thus, with a strange, poetic propriety, this earliest convert of her people was permitted to soothe by her simple, sacred ministries the last hours of this pioneer missionary in Sierra Leone.

Just after embarkation the tender shepherd had addressed his last letter to his little flock, exhorting them to continue in the grace of God. And his last intelligent and intelligible words on earth were, "I cannot live; God calls me, and this night I shall be with Him."

The tidings of his death reached the Church Missionary House in July following, and was the saddest intelligence which up to that time had ever reached that missionary center. The accounts of the wonderful work which for years had given singular occasion for joy were now followed by one awful fact of bereavement, that created a sorrow correspondingly deep. When it was learned that this apostolic missionary had departed on Sunday, May 4th, about one week after sailing, it was immediately felt that the records of his brief career in Africa must not be left to oblivion; a story of missions so instructive, so interesting, so absorbing, so profitable, must be made accessible to a large circle of readers; and so steps were taken to prepare a memoir of his life and labors, which was published in 1852.

A letter was at once sent by the secretaries at London to the native teachers at Regent's Town, breathing a most affectionate and apostolic spirit; reminding them that the hand of God was to be seen in their affliction, and that in removing their beloved human instructor He was teaching them to trust Him the more, humbling and proving them as He had done with Israel of old; and the hope was expressed that the death of their missionary pastor might be the means of turning to God many whom his preaching and life had failed to convert.

The tidings of this great bereavement found their way back to Sierra Leone in the early part of September. Of course the information spread there with telegraphic swiftness, for both grief and joy have their own quick signals for communication. In a few moments all Regent's Town was ablaze with excitement, and the mission house was at once crowded with weeping inquirers. Mr. Norman found it very difficult to assuage or even relieve their excessive grief, and could only beseech them to testify their gratitude to God for sparing so long to them their beloved teacher, by bearing with meekness and patience the trial of their faith, and by bringing forth more abundantly in their lives the fruits of the gospel. Advantage was taken of the softening influence of grief to exhort them to remember the words that he had spoken unto them while he was yet with them, and to attend faithfully to the instructions with which these seven years had been so laden. In the evening a more formal service was held in the crowded church, when the Scripture lesson for the day proved singularly appropriate: John viii. 12-19. Mr. Norman dwelt particularly on the twelfth verse: "I am the light of the world: he that followeth Me shall not walk in darkness, but shall have the light of life;" and one of the favorite hymns of the departed pastor and teacher closed the impressive service.

Knowing the strength of African emotions, Mr. Norman was both surprised and gratified at the admirably controlled behavior of this bereaved community. Their grief was deep and unmistakable, yet subdued and quiet, like a deep-flowing river; and when the service concluded, all moved out in absolute silence, restraining not only words, but even sobs.

To supply the place of the man whom God had translated to a higher sphere was no easy matter. The faith of the committee having the mission in charge was tried by severe and repeated disappointments. Mr. and Mrs. Norman were obliged to return to England in January, 1824. Eleven months passed before any resident missionary was sent to Regent's Town; and when the Rev. H. Brooks landed, he found that for want of any responsible and capable leader the public works had been stopped, the population had diminished to thirteen hundred, and there were sad signs of the need of a man of capacity and sagacity to take charge of this newly gathered church. But he also found that, notwithstanding two years of such lack of proper spiritual guidance and general superintendence, a better dressed or better behaved congregation no village even in England could show.

The death of Mr. Brooks a few weeks later again left Regent's Town without a minister. And for upward of twelve years this mission suffered from a strange succession of disappointments and calamities. As our purpose has been mainly to trace the history of the seven years of Johnson's labors, it is not needful to carry this narrative further into the subsequent years. But one incontrovertible fact stands out as bold and unmistakable as a mountain-peak against the sky. From wild, naked, wretched slaves a church and congregation had been gathered with a rapidity so astonishing, with a success so incredible, with a transformation so indescribable, that it could be traced only to the God that worketh wonders; and the companion fact that, after a lapse of more than twenty years of seeming disasters and discouragements, this congregation still remained in existence and had not relapsed into heathenism, but maintained its separation as a godly community, is a sufficient proof of the reality and solidity of the work which had been thus accomplished.

In putting the concluding paragraphs to this story of seven years of labor, we cannot forbear to observe both the coincidences and the contrasts that history presents. God raises up men to do His bidding, and provides for a true apostolic succession of witnesses, warriors, workers. At the same time in different quarters of the earth men appear, whose words shake the world, and whose lives make an ineradicable impress on the race. No human forethought could have provided for the simultaneous or coetaneous appearance of these men in history; it can be explained by nothing short of a divine Providence. And the remarkable adaptation of these different men to their spheres is a confirmatory proof that a divine hand molded these various vessels upon His potter's wheel for the exact service, in His great house, to which they were ordained.

Quite as impressive as these coincidences are the contrasts of history. Up to a certain point Luther and Loyola bear the most surprising resemblance; beyond that point it is only lifelong contrast, and a contrast of the utmost significance. Let this seven years of William Johnson at Sierra Leone be compared with the seven years of Napoleon Bonaparte between the capture of Madrid in December, 1808, and the battle of Waterloo in June, 1815. Just as Napoleon's great defeat made him a captive and exile at St. Helena, Johnson's career was about beginning in Africa. Let any candid student of history carefully set side by side the campaigns of the great Corsican and the humble evangelism of the lowly Moravian, and say which will best bear the searching eye of God, or even the fixed gaze of wise and good men. In one case a blaze of human glory, going out in disgrace and dishonor; in the other an unpretending career of service, unobserved by men, but accounted of God worthy to be accompanied by signs and seals of divine power. The man who boasted that he could "make circumstances" entered in 1812 on his Russian campaign, and actually concentrated between the Vistula and the Niemen an army of half a million. He captures Wilna, ravages Lithuania, drives before him the Russian generals, and marches directly into the snares of famine and frost. God is not on the side of his heavy battalions; in Lithuania alone one hundred thousand of his soldiers drop out of his ranks. He finds Smolensk evacuated by the enemy, but occupied by flames. At Borodino, after bloody battle, he holds the field, but nothing else. A little later he enters Moscow, but five weeks after retreats with an army reduced by nearly four fifths of its original number. He returns through the districts he had wasted in his advance, and leaves Smolensk with only forty thousand fighting men, and crosses the Beresina with only twenty-five thousand, the spell of his terrible name forever broken, and nothing but disaster before him.

William Johnson, at the time when Napoleon breathed his last at St. Helena, in 1821, had been for only five years at work in Regent's Town. Here is a man presenting, at every point, a most marked contrast to the great Corsican,—a man of no wealth, acquisitions, endowments, social standing, or education, without one element of human greatness, as men reckon greatness; out of a London workshop; having never been in college and without eloquence or learning; yet he is used of God to give organized form to a chaotic mass of human refuse, to civilize, humanize, and Christianize men and women who are little above the wild hogs that infested the district. He wins them; he weans them from their brutal, bestial vices; he builds out of them a Christian state; a well-ordered community grows up, with its streets and gardens, church and schools, homes and farms, a model of thrift, order, neatness, and industry. We find him preaching the simple news of salvation, and soon gathering fifteen hundred to two thousand hearers from among the slaves of the colony, educating one thousand in schools, and admitting four hundred to sealing ordinances. Here is found within two years a flourishing church, with crowds of sinners saved by grace and seeking to save others, and denying themselves to send the gospel to the darker parts of the continent. And when he dies, seven years after landing, and is buried at sea, every honest and honorable craft, and even the callings which demand culture and education, are represented at Regent's Town. Most wonderful of all, while the brilliant star which rose over Europe and went down in ignominious night deserves, for the incarnation of selfishness, to be known as "Wormwood," this man's whole course is one grand exhibition of the one unconscious grace, humility, and of the one celestial virtue, unselfish love. We can find not a trace of selfish ambition, appetite, avarice, in his whole labors, even when his journals and private letters are scrutinized with a critical eye. He went to Africa, not to conquer for himself, but to achieve victories for his Master. And while the church of Christ shall read the story of the miracles of missions, loving eyes will linger in wonder and amazement over the apostolic history of William Johnson and his Seven Years in Sierra Leone.*

* Appendix VII.

APPENDICES

As the original "Memoir of W. A. B. Johnson," published in 1852 in London and in 1853 in New York, is now so difficult to obtain, it seems essential to the completeness of this volume that it should include and preserve at least some of the most important and striking portions of the contents of the former narrative. Hence there will here be found seven somewhat copious extracts from the pages of that fuller and more minute account, now no longer within reach of most readers. Some of these excerpts are in themselves invaluable both as testimonies to the work and as revelations of God's gracious power.

APPENDIX I

WE extract this from Johnson's journal:

"In the evening a young man came to me and said: 'Massa, them words you talk last night strike me too much. When you preach, you read the fourteenth and fifteenth verses of the forty-fourth Isaiah, and explain them. You show how our country-people stand. Me say, "Ah, who tell massa all this? He never been in my country." You say, "Do not your country-people live in that fashion?" I say, "Yes, that true; God knows all things. He put them things in the Bible." Massa, I so sure that the Bible God's Word, for man cannot put all things there, because he no see it. That time I live in my country, I live with a man that make gree-gree. He take me into the bush and teach me to make gree-gree too. He show me one tree. He say, "That gree-gree tree." He take country ax and cut some of that tree. He make a god, and he take the leaves and that what was left, and give me to carry home. When we came home he make a fire, and all the people come and sit round the fire. Then they cook and eat. When they done eat, the man take the leaves of the gree-gree tree and burn them in the fire, and then all the people stand round the fire and clap their hands and cry, "Aha, aha!" Massa, when you read that verse, I can't tell you what I feel. You then begin to talk about the text (twentieth verse), "He feedeth on ashes;" and I was struck again, for when they done cry, "Aha," they take the ashes and make medicine; they give it to people when they be sick. You been see some gree-gree which looks like dirt; that is the same ashes they carry that our poor countrymen feed on ashes. For true the Bible God's Word. Again you talk about the twenty-first verse, and tell us to remember this, and look back and see how God pull us like brand out of the fire. Massa, I thank God for the Word I hear last night; it make my heart sorry for my country-people, but it make my heart glad when I see what God done for me. But me so wicked. God love me so much, and still my heart so cold. Massa, one thing trouble me too much: sometimes you talk about whore-mongers and adulterers. I must say I not done that sin yet, but I am so 'fraid by and by I shall do that sin. Me done that sin plenty times with my heart. I hope the Lord Jesus will have mercy upon me and keep me. Another thing trouble me; I don't know if you like to hear it, but I will tell you. My heart trouble me too much about my country-people—me so much want to be a teacher to them. I wanted to tell you before, but me so ashamed; but when you preach last night about our country-people, I think I must tell you.'"

APPENDIX II

Of the letters received by Mr. Johnson from some of the converted negroes in Sierra Leone during his stay in England, it seems proper here to give one or two. The following are selected from many:

"Regent's Town, May 26, 1819.

"My dear Father in Christ Jesus: I have written a few lines to you. I hope you are well in the Lord, and your wife. I hope you will remember me to my brethren and sisters, though I do not know them; but I trust one day or other we shall meet on the right hand of our Lord Jesus Christ.

"When I think about the office to which our Lord has appointed me, I fear.*

"When I read the Bible I learn that God said, 'Fear thou not; for I am with thee;' and, 'If ye have faith as a grain of mustard-seed, ye shall say unto this mountain, Remove hence to yonder place; and it shall remove: and nothing shall be impossible unto you.' And when I read in New Testa-

* The writer was a native assistant in one of the schools.

ment, I find Jesus said, 'He that believeth on Me hath everlasting life.' 'I am the bread of life.' This is my hope. But I fear again, because the Lord said, 'Repent, or else I will come unto thee quickly, and will fight against thee with the sword of My mouth.' This is my trouble.

"Remember me to all my brethren and sisters; let them pray for me, that the Lord may give me faith to believe in Him. I do not fear what man can do to me, for the Lord is my shield and my hope.

"Pray for me! pray for me! for I stand in need. May the grace of our Lord Jesus Christ be with you and all His children. Amen."

Another writes:

"I take this opportunity of writing these few lines unto you, my dear brother, and I hope God may preserve and keep you when you pass through the mighty deep; and, by the will of God, I hope we may see one another again. I remember you day by day, and I ask you how you feel in your heart, my dear brother. I hope you may be well in the Lord Jesus Christ—you and Mrs. Johnson; and I pray unto God that He may keep you till you come to Africa again, that we may see one another.

"I thank almighty God for his loving-kindness to me. I know the Lord is my Saviour and my God. I pray for all the good people who are in England, and the secretary. I hope you may be well in Jesus, and that you may send more missionaries to Africa to preach the gospel to our poor countrymen. My master, please to send me one hymn-book. My wife ask you, how you do, Mrs. Johnson?"

The writer of one of these letters gives the following affecting account of the state of the colony during the few months preceding. The feelings of the Christian natives under their bereavements afford a fair indication of the value of the mission.

"I stayed at Charlotte Town when Mr. Taylor was sick, and I speak to the people the Word of God. One time we meet together for missionary prayer-meeting. Oh, that time many white people sick, and many of them die!

"And that time we lose one of our sisters, Mary Moddy; she was brought to bed, and the child died, and herself caught cold. And I went to see her, and I asked her, 'How you do?' She said, 'I fear too much.' I asked her, 'What you fear for?' And she said, 'I done sin.' And I said, 'Pray to the Lord Jesus Christ; He only can do you good.' And I prayed with her, and the next day I went again, and I say unto her, 'How do you feel in your heart?' And she said, 'Oh, my heart too wicked!' And I said, 'Do you pray to Jesus Christ?' She said, 'Yes; to whom should I pray, if I not pray to the Lord Jesus Christ?' And I talked with her a good while, and then I prayed with her and went away. The next day I went again, and she could hardly speak. I prayed with her, and stop with her, and by and by she died.

"That time Mr. Cates sick, and Mr. Morgan sick, and poor Mr. Cates die. I think the journey to the Bassa country which he take, that too much for him, the land so long to walk and the sun so hot. Yet I cannot prove that; but I think his work was done and his time up. When he was sick I went to see him. 'How do you do, Mr. Cates?' And he said, 'I shall certainly die.' And by and by he got down to Freetown, and he sink very much—all his strength gone; but he was a man of faith, and he die on Friday about five o'clock. And on Saturday we go to bury him four o'clock, and we look upon him; and then we went to Mr. Jesty's house, and Mr. Jesty tell us, and say, he think God would leave this place, because white people die fast; and when I hear that I fear too much, and I consider many things in my mind; and I think hypocrites live among us, and God want to punish us; but I trust again in the Lord; He knows His people, He never forsake them. Then Mr. Collier get sick, and Mr. Morgan get sick again; and our friend said, 'God soon leave this place.' And I said, 'I trust in the Lord Jesus Christ; He knows His people, and He never left them, neither forsake them.' And next Sunday Mr. Collier die about eleven o'clock. Then Mr. Morgan sick, Mrs. Morgan sick, Mr. Bull sick! Oh, that time all missionaries sick! We went to Freetown Monday, bury Mr. Collier, and we come home again and keep service in the church. Oh, that time trouble too much in my heart! Nobody to teach me, and I was sorry for my poor country-people. Mr. Cates died, Mr. Collier died, Mr. Morgan sick! Oh, what must I do for my countrymen? But I trust in the Lord Jesus Christ, He know what to do; and I went to pray, and I say, 'O Lord, take not all the teachers away from us.'"

APPENDIX III

MR. THOMAS MORGAN TO THE SECRETARY

" . . . I HAD in England read, heard, and thought much on the African character, or rather given in to some prejudices against the mental endowments of the negroes, and leaning rather still to the side of uncharitableness. On my arrival I resolved to study, as much as possible, a particular acquaintance with their private thoughts; and I now find, from summing up the various occurrences which I have myself witnessed, you have reason to adore God for suffering you to open a door through which the light of the Sun of righteousness is now spreading its influence over the whole country of Ethiopia.

"No blame can attach itself to any missionary or superintendent for not becoming acquainted with every occurrence which happens among the negroes entrusted to their care. Their labors, were they to do nothing more than absolute duty, and what the world, indifferent to the people's eternal interests, would expect, are truly great, difficult, and arduous; and if, with your departed servant,[*] I visited the members of each family separately, it was to gratify my own inclination, and to try the ground of those faults so often assigned to professing Christian negroes. Faults and crimes were found, and many were great; but none surpassed, nor did they equal, the state of the towns of the same size, and which for centuries have heard and read the gospel, in England. This is a proof that African towns (I speak especially of Regent's Town) are superior to the towns of England in moral and religious conduct; and if we take into view the short period since civilization began here, we may say it is a light to the people of Britain. They who in Africa have sat in darkness have seen a great light, and it hath shined into their hearts.

"I have mentioned in former letters the ultimate success which attended my exertions in Freetown schools. I have seen there Dr. Bell's remark veri-

---
[*] Mr. Cates.

fied. A child of any ability may with facility proceed from reading the alphabet to the reading of the Bible in four months. This leads me to offer a remark on the ability of the negroes. If I can recollect my own at an early period of life, theirs is as far superior as one child need wish to be to another. A strong barrier this for those to conquer who think them only fit to labor for the gratification of their owners. I wish every heart which undervalues the character of these poor heathen could have visited them with me, have seen their labors of love and imitated their zeal for religion.

"Soon after my arrival at Regent's Town, Mrs. Morgan and myself were both seized with the fever, in which we were tenderly and unceasingly watched by the children around us. As I often suffered much in my head, and, I believe, frequently manifested it by contortion of countenance, a boy, who had attached himself to me from his first entering the colony, and whom I kept constantly about me, sat for several hours in the night holding my head and bathing it with vinegar, and, when I dropped asleep, covering it from cold or wiping away the drops of perspiration. No affection, I think, in a Christian land would surpass this.

"One morning in the month of June, and during Mrs. Morgan's indisposition, Brother Cates and myself being engaged, as was our custom at breakfast, in reading Milner's 'Church History,' we were alarmed by feeble cries of 'Massa, massa, fire live here!' I went immediately to the adjoining room, and found the flames issuing through the crevices of the floor. Brother Cates followed, and with his usual self-possession and calmness said, 'We will remove this child' (who was lying sick in the room) 'and Mrs. Morgan; and God will assist us to get the fire under.' This we accordingly did, and by the application of wet blankets soon confined and at last extinguished the fire.

"We were much struck with the *integrity* of the people. In their anxiety to save as much as possible, almost every article was removed. In the confusion many things were scattered about the yard; not one article, however, even the most trifling, was lost, but all were brought again to the house and fixed in their proper places. A boy who had got possession of the box which contained the money for paying the mechanics and laborers was found in the garden, parading with the box under his arm, and guarding it, though unnecessarily, with a drawn cutlass in his hand.

"I was struck, during a fire which broke out in our house, with the sudden disappearance of the women, who at the commencement almost filled the house. On inquiry I found that they had retired to the church to offer up their prayers unto God. What but a divine influence could draw them to God in this trial, to ask His blessing on the exertions of those employed?

"While we were replacing the books which had been scattered on this occasion, two of the girls came to us. I asked what was wanted. 'Nothing, massa,' was the reply; 'but we come tell you God hear every time somebody go talk Him.' 'How, my child,' said I, 'do you know that God hears His people when they pray?' She said, 'Massa, when fire come this morning I sabby your house no burn too much. Every morning I hear you and Mr. Cates, and you pray God keep this house and all them girls and boys what live here; and when fire come I say to Sarah, "Ah! God plenty good; He heard what massa say to Him this morning; He no let this house burn too much."' What a reproof did I feel this! I knew how often my heart was indifferent while I asked for these mercies; and I trust it made me more anxious to urge the duty of family prayer on others more earnestly. Soon after the same girls mentioned their desire for one of the elder girls to pray with the school-children before they went to bed and when they rose in the morning.

"Scarcely an event occurs but what they notice as springing from the overruling providence of God. Taught of God, they mark the painful events of His providence, as children would mark the dealings of a father. After the death of Mr. Cates I have frequently heard their expressions of sorrow for sin, and acknowledgments of God's justice in punishing them. They have used such language as this: 'We have done something very bad—God is very angry; He is removing all our teachers; by and by nobody will be left to tell us good. We must pray, dear brothers and sisters; we must look into our own hearts; some bad live there.' Similar occurrences in England would have passed, perhaps, unheeded by the greater part of professing Christians.

"How many candlesticks spreading around them the light of truth, and reflecting the rays of Him who fed their luster by His own incomprehensible glory, are removed from the congregation where Jesus had planted them, without giving rise to the thought, 'God is angry with us for sin'! What has not our God permitted your society to do already? What a call to go forward and increase in the work!

"No day passed, when I was capable of taking exercise, without my entering some of the huts around us. Visiting unexpectedly, as I often did, the families of all classes of the communicants, I could not be deceived as to their actual condition.

"I have found many commendably employed in agriculture. I believe the society is apt to conceive that a cultivated farm or garden in Africa must resemble the same thing in England, which it does not. I have often myself drawn too strong a line of comparison between the two. Agriculture is, among many, especially those on whose hearts we trust the dew of God's grace is continually descending, flourishing.

"Many of the gardens are kept in very neat order, though most of the owners have but little leisure to devote to this employment. I have frequently known the whole of the time allowed for dinner spent by both husband and wife in fencing, digging, or planting the little spot of ground attached to each dwelling.

"Decency and cleanliness manifest the diligence of those who live under the power of religion. Their time is, indeed, so well occupied that in cases where they can read they may be frequently seen at leisure moments with some friends around them searching the Word of life; and these little respites from labor are often made a blessing to the whole town, as the sick, the careless, the backsliding, and the profane are not seldom visited, instructed, warned, comforted, and relieved at these seasons by their zealous brethren.

"The Christian negroes show a strong attachment to the simplest views of religion. I began some explanation as plain as possible, in successive evenings, of the Lord's Prayer. It pleased God graciously to bless these words to the people. They made the most practical use of them. A display of an unholy temper would receive a reproof: 'If God your Father, that be no like His child.' Some said that they needed indeed such a Father; others, such daily bread. Some thought God could not be their

Father, because they did not feel sufficient desires that His kingdom should come among their country-people; and others felt that they were rebellious children for not doing His will on earth more as it was done in heaven. Some wept to think how He delivered them from temptation and evil; and all, I believe, burned with love to ascribe to him the kingdom of His love, the power of His Spirit, and the glory of their salvation.

"I was obliged, by the pressing requests of the people, to repeat these explanations four or five times, and resolved in future to know nothing and to speak of nothing among the negroes but the plainest words of the Redeemer. How much better calculated His language is than any other to reach the heart may be judged of by this instance out of many.

"How much may be gained by the simplicity, or rather sublimity, of the gospel, I never knew before. The work in which the missionary engages must be the work of Jesus, for He suits and opens every capacity to receive heavenly manna.

"But there was another reason which tended to render this subject useful. I had it frequently read before I spoke on it, which proves how rapidly, under God's blessing, the knowledge of the gospel must increase if the soil wherein the grain is cast were more cultivated and manured by acquaintance with the Bible. Difficulties, I know, are great, and the man who goes as a schoolmaster to labor among the heathen must expect many trials on earth. However the comprehension of the minds of the Africans may be ridiculed, I have found them, though needing cultivation, far from barren. The finer feelings of the soul in the attachment of these people to their instructors, families, and friends are equal to the sons and daughters of the princes of Europe.

"How eminently the gospel shines in the conduct of the people, and how strikingly its influence is manifested, no one can possibly conjecture but those who have been eye-witnesses. I have frequently experienced myself, and seen experienced by different superintendents, the most docile and tractable dispositions.

"On the disbanding of the West India regiments sent to the colony for that purpose, a natural degree of affectionate feeling was excited in the breasts of the negroes to see them. These regiments had been several years before formed of liberated negroes, and many of the people were expecting to find parents, brothers, and friends among them. The feelings of glowing hope were strongly delineated in almost every countenance. When in the evening intelligence arrived that on the following morning the troops would be permitted to land, after evening prayer it became a matter of general conversation. Some were looking forward with hope, while their joy cast a cloud over the faces of others, whose friends had been murdered in different skirmishes when they themselves were enslaved. In the morning, at prayer, the church was particularly full, and a few words were spoken on the danger to which a Christian was exposed when running into temptation, and some desire intimated that none would visit Freetown that day. I gave this intimation against my own feelings; for I thought their wishes laudable, though I feared the consequences which might arise from gratifying them. In the course of an hour after, an old and faithful Christian came to tell me that his brother was come among the soldiers. 'Well,' said I, 'and do you wish to see him?' 'Yes, massa, I want to look him, but I no want to go to-day.' 'Well,' I replied, 'I want to send to Freetown; if you can find another communicant who wishes to go and see the soldiers, I will send you down.' After a search of near two hours he returned with: 'Well, massa, me no find one that want to go; all them people what belong to church think 'tis no good for them to run where God say temptation live.' Two days elapsed before this poor fellow, whose heart was full of affection to his brother, went to Freetown to see him. I singled him out as a fit object of reward; and having mentioned the subject to the governor, that father of the liberated negroes, anticipating my request, promised, and kept his promise, that the brothers should have the privilege of living together.

"I know of many similar instances, but this one struck me much. I thought it an example worthy of imitation, and was fully convinced that while I had known the gospel longer I had obeyed it less.

"You must think that, more than according to the labors of the society, God has blessed. The church has much reason to take up David's exclamation, and say, 'Bless the Lord, O my soul, and forget not all His benefits.' There are, as must be expected, many errors in large towns, but the good which has been done in Africa neither we nor the generations to come will be able to fathom. Perhaps never one of your servants ever noticed the field of your labors with more impartial views than did my dear Brother Cates and myself; and it was not till I had left that field that I suffered my mind to form a sentiment on the subject."

APPENDIX IV

Of a Sunday spent at Regent's Town, Mr. Jesty, after speaking of an early meeting in the church, at six o'clock in the morning, thus writes:

"At ten o'clock I saw a sight which at once astonished and delighted me. The bell at the church rung for divine service, on which Mr. Johnson's well-regulated schools of boys and girls walked, two and two, to the church—the girls extremely clean, and dressed entirely in white, in striking contrast with which were their black arms and faces; the boys, equally clean, were dressed in white trousers and scarlet jackets. The clothing of both boys and girls is supplied by government.

"The eagerness of the inhabitants to hear the Word will appear from their early attendance on the means of grace. It is true, there is a bell in the steeple of the church, but it is of little use at Regent's Town, for the church is generally filled half an hour before the bell tolls. The greatest attention is paid during the service. Indeed, I witnessed a Christian congregation in a heathen land—a people 'fearing God and working righteousness.' The tear of godly sorrow rolled down many a colored cheek, and showed the contrition of a heart that felt its own vileness.

"At three o'clock in the afternoon there was again a very full attendance, so that scarce an individual was to be seen throughout the town, so eager are they to hear the Word, and to feed on that 'living bread that came down from heaven.' The service was over about half-past four o'clock.

"At six we met again; and although many had to come from a considerable distance, and up a tremendous hill, I did not perceive any decrease of number, or any weariness in their frequent attendance on the means of grace.

"We left the church about eight o'clock, and returned to Mr. Johnson's house, which is close by the church. While at supper I heard singing, and on walking into the piazza found that about twenty of the school-girls were assembled under it. One of the elder girls gave out the hymn in an impressive manner, while a younger girl held a lamp. After we had supped, the girls, in a very respectful and humble way, sent up to Mr. Johnson to know if he would allow them to come upstairs into his sitting-room, to sing a parting hymn. On their entering the room Mr. Johnson gave out a hymn, and in a few minutes I think we had at least one hundred and twenty boys and girls in the room and piazza. They sang three hymns; and after a few suitable words from Mr. Johnson they departed, pleased with the favor granted them.

"Thus was the last Sabbath spent in Regent's Town. Never did I pass such a day in my dear native country. Never did I witness such a congregation in a professing Christian land, nor ever beheld such apparent sincerity and brotherly love."

Of the monthly meeting, held on the following evening, Mr. Jesty thus writes:

"Mr. Johnson and myself entered the names of subscribers and received their mites; and I cannot but notice that, in one minute after Mr. Johnson and myself were ready to receive the money and names, we were surrounded by several hundreds of humble friends to missionary exertions, crying, as it were with one voice, 'Massa, take my money!' 'Massa, massa, take mine!' 'Eight coppers one moon.' It was indeed a pleasing sight to behold a people—once led captive at the will of Satan, devoted to gross superstition and folly, embracing their gree-grees and trusting in them for defense, and once expending all the money that they could spare in the purchase of these false gods—now conquered by the love and power of Him that taketh away the sin of the world, and with cheerful and renewed hearts giving of their little substance to aid those means which, by the blessing of God, will communicate the privileges of the gospel to their countrymen also.

"From these few poor and once injured and despised Africans we collected that evening about £2. 7s. O my countrymen, fellow-Christians in highly favored England, you who have multiplied and daily renewed comforts and blessings, 'go and do likewise'!"

Of the manner of closing this day Mr. Jesty says:

"After we left the church the children of the two schools retired to their school-houses, and the rest of the congregation to their respective homes.

"But that faith which cometh from above and worketh by love has taken such possession of the hearts of this people, that they delight to be continually 'speaking one to another in psalms and hymns and spiritual songs, and to sing with grace in their hearts to the Lord.'

"The school-houses are situated behind Mr. Johnson's, on a higher part of the hill. The school-girls assembled in a row before their school-house, with three or four lamps dispersed through the line. Their eldest teacher gave out the hymn, and they were singing delightfully:

> 'How beauteous are their feet,
> Who stand on Zion's hill!'

While the girls were singing this hymn the boys had climbed a little higher up the hill, when one of their teachers gave out the hymn:

> 'Come, ye sinners, poor and wretched!'

"It was a beautiful moonlight night, so that the children could be seen from all parts of the town, while the lofty mountains resounded with the echo of their voices. I was walking up and down in the piazza listening to them, and anticipating the time when all kings shall fall down before the Redeemer and all nations shall serve Him, when I saw at the foot of the hill some men and women coming toward the children. The men joined the boys, and the women joined the girls.

"The boys and girls had now sung several hymns, and after a few minutes' cessation began again. I was thinking of our Christian friends in England, and said to Mr. Johnson, 'Could all the friends of missionary exertions but witness this scene, they would be more and more zealous for the universal diffusion of the gospel of a crucified Saviour,'—when I looked around me and saw numbers of the inhabitants, men and women, coming in every direction. They joined respectively the boys and girls, and sang for some time, when the boys and girls retired to their school-houses, and the men and women retired to their homes in peace.

"This is a great work, and it is marvelous in our eyes; but it is the Lord, and to Him be all the glory!"

Mr. Jesty adds:

"We rose next morning between five and six o'clock, and attended morning prayer at the church. After the service was over a few more came forward, and begged us to take their coppers to aid the cause of missions. We collected on this occasion upward of fifteen shillings, which, with the collection made the evening before, amounted to more than three pounds. Mr. Johnson has a missionary meeting and sermon once a month, on which occasions he generally collects three pounds. Do not these poor people hold forth a bright example to all Christians?

"I have now given you a faithful and imperfect picture of the state of Regent's Town. The Lord has certainly blessed, in a peculiar manner, the labors of Mr. Johnson. The people love him as their father, and reverence him as their spiritual guide. Should a dispute arise among any of them, they come to him to settle their palaver, and they abide by his decision. He seems in every respect suited for these people—unwearied in his exertions, and an excellent example to all his brethren."

Mrs. Jesty thus concludes her letter to her sister:

"The love which these people manifest among themselves, and toward their minister and all faithful missionaries, their anxiety and the fervency of their prayers that the gospel may be made known through all nations—these things are worthy the admiration of all Christians. It may almost be said of the inhabitants of Regent's Town that they 'dwell in love,' and that they live a life of prayer and praise to Him 'who loved them, and gave Himself for them'; for besides their meetings for prayer every morning and evening, the hearts of many of them seem to be full of the love of Christ the whole day; and when 'they are merry they sing psalms'; such vocal music resounds from all parts of the town. A dispute is seldom known among them. They have every one of them cast off his gree-gree, and nearly all of them are become worshipers of the blessed Jesus. A few years since none of the inhabitants of this place had ever heard the name of Jesus; they went about naked, and were in every respect like the savage tribes; but now—oh, what a happy change!—they are all decently dressed; and it is the most heart-cheering sight to see them flock together in crowds to the house of prayer.

"Mr. Johnson has been made an instrument of incalculable good to this people. Under his ministry one hundred and sixteen persons have become communicants, and one hundred and ten are candidates for baptism and the Lord's Supper; these will be received as members of the church of Christ on Easter Sunday. He is very particular in his examination of the people before they are admitted to the Lord's table.

"It may indeed be said that 'numbers are added to the church daily'; for Mr. Johnson has frequently five or six in a day coming to his house to talk of the state of their souls, who appear to be very sincere. During the few days that we have been here, upward of fifty persons have been to tell Mr. Johnson of their troubles, which they confess in affecting terms: 'My bad heart trouble me, me no sleep all night; me no peace, me know me very wicked, but God good too much; me t'ank God for what He done for my soul; me want love Jesus more; me want to go to Jesus; me know nothing else but de blood of Jesus can wash away my sin.' Such complaints as those from these lost sheep of Israel are incessantly brought before their worthy pastor, who with affection directs them to the great Comforter, and advises them to embrace that gospel which is 'the power of God unto salvation.'

"O my dear sister, is not this encouraging to all Christian friends in England to be doubly zealous and active in their missionary exertions? Let me entreat you all to be unwearied in your efforts and prayers, that all Africa may become as Regent's Town. This is the fruit of the gospel. Oh, send forth the gospel and more faithful laborers into the vineyard of the Lord! Let me again beg of you, my dear sister, to 'pray and not to faint.' Let the interests of Christ's kingdom be ever uppermost in your heart. Here is yet a wide field for labor. May the happy effect of the gospel be felt by all benighted Africa, and to God shall the glory be given forever."

APPENDIX V

Mr. Singleton thus writes of Regent's Town:

"The population of Regent's Town is about 1350; of this number, 700 are able to provide for themselves and families by means of their farms. One man sold the produce of his little spot last year for fifty pounds, and the quantity of cassava sold then was ten thousand bushels.

"A small market is held each day, but the seventh day is the principal one. Five oxen are weekly consumed, besides pork.

"The people, with a few exceptions, are industrious, as may be seen by the improved houses which they build for themselves, by their furniture, all of their own making, and by the neatness and cleanliness of their habitations. In several houses are sofas covered with clean print or the country cloth, tables and forms, or chairs; and especially I noticed in each house a corner cupboard with its appropriate crockery ware. The beds and sleeping-rooms are remarkably neat and clean. A few of the inhabitants, more ingenious or richer than the rest, are building houses of board, with stores below and piazza in front.

"The superintendent appears to have considerable influence with the people, and his advice is readily followed.

"A woman whose husband absconded about four years since, and has not been heard of during that time, asked the superintendent some time after the man's departure if she might not marry again; he informed her that the law of England required a period of seven years before that was allowed. She submitted, and to the present has lived alone, maintaining herself and acting with exemplary propriety.

"As we were standing under the piazza this morning (sixth day), a young African came to ask permission to marry. W. Johnson gave good reasons for withholding his assent, which he had scarcely done when he was called away; and I advised the hesitating youth to acquiesce. He readily answered: 'My massa good man. He say girl too young. We wait. I no pass de word of my massa.'

"Returning from a walk over one or two of the farms, and coming near the market-place, we were met by an elderly African, with a basket on his head covered with a cloth. He stopped, and, placing the basket on the ground, drew out a glass bottle, which he held up that the superintendent might see its contents, and uttered a few words which I could not understand. The bottle contained palm-wine; and the man in his simplicity produced it uncalled for, to assure the superintendent that it was not rum, the use of this liquor being prohibited.

"Soon after breakfast Captain Grant came in. We visited the schools together. The girls behaved with seriousness, and appeared under good care. There was an agreeable solidity in their countenances which, I hope, indicated something good within. The boys were attentive, and the monitors active, as was the case too at Gloucester and Kissy.

"I visited with satisfaction the school at Freetown and those at several of the villages in the mountains. At Regent's Town I remained two days, and left the family and villagers with regret. This is a favored place, and while there I indulged in a wish that if the Friends should be induced to commence a settlement on the Gambia, their success might equal that of the superintendent of Regent's Town."

APPENDIX VI

Mr. Bacon published on his return to Philadelphia an account of his visit to Africa, containing the following sketch of Regent's Town:
"March 17, 1821, Saturday. About one o'clock we arrived at Regent's Town. Mr. and Mrs. Johnson had been at Freetown, where Mr. Johnson was sick several weeks. On our arrival great numbers of his people came to shake hands with him, and inquired affectionately after his health. The expression of every countenance bore strong testimony of their ardent love for him, and of the joy which filled their hearts on his recovery from sickness and his safe return to his flock.

"At six o'clock in the evening the bell at the church rang for divine service. The people were immediately seen walking from different parts of the town, the parsonage house being so situated that there is a fair view of almost the whole settlement; and it was delightful to observe the eagerness which the people manifested to hear the Word of God. A prayer-meeting was held by the communicants after the usual evening prayers, it being expected that the Lord's Supper would be celebrated the next day.

"March 18th, Sunday. At six o'clock the bell rang for morning prayers, when the church was again filled. How pleasing to behold hundreds of those who were once wretched inmates of the holds of slave-ships assembled in the house of God on the morning of that holy day on which our blessed Saviour rose from the dead and ascended up to heaven! With a hundred copies of the Holy Bible spread open before their black faces, their eyes were fixed intently on the words of the lesson which their godly pastor was reading. Almost all Mr. Johnson's people who can read the blessed book are supplied with Bibles from that best of institutions, the British and Foreign Bible Society. Surely Christians ought to feel themselves encouraged in the support of missions when such cheering fruits present themselves to view!

"At ten o'clock the bell again rang, though the church was nearly filled before that hour. The members of the well-regulated schools, which passed in review before the parsonage in regular succession, were all clad in clean and decent apparel. When we arrived at the church there were no vacant seats to be seen. The greatest attention was paid during divine service. 'Indeed, I witnessed a Christian congregation in a heathen land—a people "fearing God and working righteousness." The tear of godly sorrow rolled down many a colored cheek, and showed the contrition of a heart that felt its own vileness.' There were three couples married and one child baptized. After the sermon Mr. Johnson, with the assistance of Brother Andrus, administered the communion of the body and blood of our Lord Jesus Christ to nearly four hundred communicants. This indeed was 'a feast of fat things' to my soul.

"At three o'clock the church was again filled, and the most devout attention was paid to the reading and hearing of the Word. The whole congregation seemed eager to catch every word which fell from the pastor's lips.

"Again, before the ringing of the bell at six o'clock in the evening, the people were seen from the distant parts of the town leaving their homes, and retracing their steps toward the house of God. There we again united in praising that God who hath wrought such wonderful things even among the mountains of Sierra Leone, where the praises of Jehovah resound not only from His holy sanctuary, but from the humblest mud-walled cottage— from the tongues of those children of Africa who have been taken by the avaricious slave-trader, dragged from parents, separated from brother and sister, and perhaps from wife or husband, bound in chains, hurried on board the slave-ship, crowded in a space not exceeding their length and breadth, nor even allowed to breathe the vital air. These persons, after being recaptured by order of the British government, have been put under the charge of a faithful minister of the gospel, whose labors have been accompanied by the Holy Spirit. These are the mighty works of God."

APPENDIX VII

The original memoir of Johnson thus impressively concludes:

"And now we bring our narrative to a close. The lessons it teaches are many; but two or three thoughts more immediately present themselves.

"The first is, the sovereignty and power which mark certain of the divine operations.

"It was remarked a few years since by an aged and thoughtful minister: 'We do the best we can to raise up a succession of faithful ministers of the gospel. We look out for young men of promise— men whose hearts God seems to have touched; we put them under instruction; we make them theologians and preachers; and thus whatever is in our power we do, and in so doing we act rightly; no other course is open to us. To a certain degree we succeed, though we often have to mourn over grievous disappointments. But now and then it pleases God to take the work into His own hands. He raises up a man, and makes him a preacher of the gospel by His own especial teaching, and *then* we behold a very different sort of minister from any that human efforts or human skill can produce.'

"The truth of this remark, which was uttered long before either of these remarkable men had been given to the Christian church, has since been made strikingly evident in the histories of Williams and of Johnson. No two individuals in modern times have been so honored of God in the missionary work as were these two men, and none could be more evidently prepared by Himself for the work.

"It was in the year 1816—a year which will be ever memorable in the angelic annals—that the mission of these two men was commanded. An eminent prelate of our church once compared Mr. Williams's narratives with the Acts of the Apostles,* and under such sanction we cannot hesitate to say that, as in A.D. 45 (Acts xiii. 2) so in A.D. 1816, 'the Holy Ghost said, Separate Me Johnson and Williams for the work whereunto I have called them.' And what was that work? It was one as absolutely beyond all human power as was the subjection of the Roman empire to the sway of Him who was crucified on Calvary.

"Two regions of the earth were preëminently reigned over by the Evil One. In Africa, among the degraded race of Ham, the slave-trade had done its work in crushing, brutalizing, exterminating, while their religion was avowedly *devil-worship*. In Polynesia some of the most lovely spots on the earth were becoming depopulated by vice and unnatural

* The late Bishop of Ripon, who called these narratives the "twenty-ninth chapter of the Acts."—A. T. P.

cruelty. Mothers slept calmly on beds beneath which they had buried many of their own murdered infants. Over these two regions Satan ruled supreme, and his kingdom of hell was almost visibly established. To overthrow that dominion it pleased God to send forth two young men—not a phalanx of learned theologians or well-taught divines or clever and astute philosophers, but two men of no learning, possessing only a scanty measure of the most ordinary instruction. There cannot be a doubt that this was ordered as in the apostle's day: 'After that . . . the world by wisdom knew not God, it pleased God by the foolishness of preaching to save them that believe. . . . Because the foolishness of God is wiser than men; and the weakness of God is stronger than men' (1 Cor. i. 21, 25).

"Had the event proved otherwise, the directors of the London Missionary Society would have been deemed by many to have laid themselves open to censure. John Williams had not arrived at the age of manhood when he was sent forth, and his previous instruction had occupied but a few short months.

"As to William Johnson, he had been a mechanic; had been placed in the National Society's training-school for a single twelvemonth, and was sent forth by the Church Missionary Society to labor in West Africa as a schoolmaster. It is quite certain that neither of these societies had an idea, when they sent forth these young men with far less than the ordinary preparation, what important instruments, in the hand of the Holy Ghost, they were then dismissing to their labors.

"But, though called to the work at about the same period and sent forth in the same year, and resembling each other greatly in their previous histories, there was a wide difference in the two spheres of labor for which they were destined, and there was a similar difference in the character of their minds. He who 'knew what was in man,' and who 'fashioneth the clay like a potter,' gave to Polynesia the conqueror and civilizer, Williams, and to oppressed Africa the sympathizing consoler and preacher, Johnson. The same gospel dwelt in the hearts and on the lips of each, but the outward circumstances of their respective missions were very different. Mr. Williams's lot was cast in a land

> 'Where every prospect pleases,
> And only *man* is vile.'

Luxury, indolence, and luxurious vice were the foes with which he had to wrestle. What a picture of the native opulence of those regions is given by the single fact that the people of one of those islands, few in number, were able, when really awakened to their duty, to send home to the parent society in one year a contribution of the value of *eighteen hundred pounds!*

"It is no detraction from the merits of Mr. Williams to remark that Mr. Johnson, placed in more painful and difficult circumstances, shines under these circumstances with a still brighter light. Ease and luxury, sunny climes and softening atmospheres, are not those which are most favorable to Christian heroism. Multitudes of predecessors in the missionary work had sunk under these temptations, and had failed in the same undertaking in which Mr. Williams so remarkably succeeded. The difficulties which surrounded Mr. Johnson were of a different class. The climate, it is true, was in each case unfavorable to vigorous effort; but, while surrounding circumstances in Polynesia almost resembled those of Bunyan's 'enchanted ground,' the case of a missionary in western Africa was widely different. Despondency might coöperate with a relaxing climate, and so produce a despairing inertness; but assuredly everything around was replete with painful sights and dread-inspiring alarms. Poverty, degradation, physical and moral wretchedness among the people, conspired, with frequent sickness and death among the laborers, to throw the missionary upon his God as his only refuge and strength, 'a very present help in time of trouble.' And *when* this result was produced, the effect was naturally most salutary. It recalled Cowper's lines:

> 'For He who knew what human hearts would prove,—
> How slow to learn the dictates of His love;
> That, hard by nature and of stubborn will,
> A life of ease would make them harder still,—
> In pity to the souls His grace designed
> To rescue from the ruins of mankind,
> Called for a cloud to darken all their years,
> And said, "Go, spend them in the vale of tears."'

"The general effect, then, of these differing circumstances was, that while both these eminent men preached the same gospel, and with the same simplicity and faithfulness, the results were modified by external influences. In Mr. Williams's case we find large and rapid successes; in Mr. Johnson's, more limited but perhaps more deeply spiritual conversions. We remark the difference not in depreciation of Mr. Williams's labors; had he been placed in Mr. Johnson's circumstances he would probably have been what Mr. Johnson was; while Mr. Johnson, in Polynesia, would have proved himself another Williams. 'But all these worketh that one and the selfsame Spirit, dividing to every man severally as He will' (1 Cor. xii. 11). Nor must the reader forget, in comparing these two eminently successful missionaries, that Mr. Williams's course was prolonged to more than two and twenty years, while Mr. Johnson's ended in less than seven.

"A second remark which naturally suggests itself is this: that when God speaks to any man *directly*, as He spoke to William Johnson, the speech of that man to his fellow-sinners will often be found to be similarly *direct* and effective.

"Johnson was awakened and called 'out of darkness into marvelous light' without human instrumentality. By the Holy Ghost, working with conspiring circumstances, his heart was penetrated. The preacher's part which followed was only to administer comfort and to point to Christ. And when so built upon the only sure foundation, and made desirous of spreading the knowledge of salvation, it is most worthy of remark that he could scarcely open his mouth without some one being stricken to the heart. The proofs of the directness and effective character of his preaching pervade his whole history. The 'live coal from the altar' evidently had 'touched his lips,' and his speech was 'with demonstration of the Spirit and with power.'

"One more observation must be made, though with fear and trembling. In the short but eminently successful career of Mr. Johnson, we see how practicable it is to unite a burning zeal with a sound judgment, and how excellently the two combine to form the able minister of the gospel.

"In the present day, prudence and caution and decorum are more common than fervency and earnest zeal; and hence it follows that any overflowing of earnestness is almost sure to be checked and reproved, as 'bordering on enthusiasm.' It was so in Mr. Johnson's case. His very first step in his public duty exposed him to such a check; but a review of his whole course presents him in the light of one who merely felt and acted in the spirit of St. Paul. He was willing to be 'made all things to all men, that he might *by all means* save some.' He was 'instant in season, *out of season*, reproving, rebuking, exhorting with all long-suffering and doctrine.' But he was ever watchful, humble, desirous to receive the counsel of his elders, and prompt in obeying it. He kept an even course between the urgency of the governor, on the one hand, desirous of a general admission into the church, and the apprehensions, on the other, of 'that fearful Tamba, dreading that the church would be filled with hypocrites.' The soundness of his judgment and the wisdom of his course are seen in the rapid disappearance of disorder, and the perpetual increase of his influence over his people. Not by mere priestly pretensions, but by the legitimate sway of mind over mind and heart over heart, he won his way, till toward the close of his course the control exercised by him seemed all that a pastor could desire. It is not indeed to be doubted that, as in the apostolic churches, so in Regent's Town, the enemy was sedulously employed in sowing tares among the wheat. We have already seen that within a few weeks after his departure the temptation of ardent spirits crept in. If we had pursued the story still later, we might have met with the sad story of a quarrel, ending with the appearance of some of the Regent's Town communicants, as criminals, before a magistrate. But the counterpart of all this had been written before, in St. Paul's and St. Peter's epistles (2 Cor. xii. 21; 2 Pet. ii. 18–22). And the best criterion of Mr. Johnson's having followed Paul, as Paul followed his Master, is that his whole narrative bears the closest resemblance to the apostle's own experience, as we find it depicted in his various epistles.

"Such is the work of God, carried on by a few of His people, for 'accomplishing the number of His elect and hastening His kingdom.' Let us compare it, for a few moments, with some of the works of man.

"And the contrast which first and most naturally presents itself is that of such a mission as Regent's Town with the missions of Rome.

"All the missions of which Rome boasts have been enterprises begun and carried on within the last three centuries. And whatever the Roman Church might have been in earlier times, we believe that from the Reformation downward, at least, it has been apostate, and its works, therefore, the works of fallen man and not of God. Let us compare those works with a Protestant mission such as that of Regent's Town.

"We have here the narrative of a plain and simple mechanic, educated but scantily for a schoolmaster of poor liberated negroes, but who, in the course of his labors, speaking of Christ to them, becomes the means of building up an extensive Christian church. Very soon we find him assembling fifteen hundred people together, Sunday by Sunday, admitting four hundred of them to the Lord's table, and educating one thousand in schools. The reality of the work is shown by its endurance. After much adversity and many discouragements long continued, Regent's Town at this moment rejoices in the Christian church which was founded by William Johnson. From that church many redeemed souls have joined the blessed company in paradise. Now a parallel to all this may be found in other Christian missions, such as those of Mr. Williams, already alluded to, the churches gathered by the Moravians in different countries, and the churches now multiplying in Tinnevelly. But is the like to be found in the history of the papal church? There are indeed large records of their successes, and we believe that, at various periods, the missionaries of Rome in divers countries have succeeded in *baptizing* great numbers. To baptize myriads of ignorant and unconverted heathens, however, if this be all, is a mere delusion. Has there been, among the annals of Romish missions, a single instance resembling that of Regent's Town in its *reality*—a single instance, we mean, of a Christian congregation not only *baptized*, but brought into the habits, feelings, and tempers of the Christian life? We have met with no such history, and we doubt if such a one exists.

"But we may pass from the counterfeit Christianity of apostate Rome to the other religions of mankind. Do we find among them anything resembling a genuine Christian mission, either in its self-sacrifice or in its wondrous results?

"'Look at the spirit of aggression which characterizes this religion, its undeniable power to prompt those who hold it to render it *victorious*—a spirit which has not been least active in our own time. We do not see anything like this in other religions. We do not see mollas from Ispahan, Brahmans from Benares, bonzes from China, preaching *their* systems of religion in London, Paris, and Berlin, supported, year after year, by an enormous expenditure on the part of their zealous compatriots, and the nations who support them taking the liveliest interest in their success or failure.'* In fact, it is Christianity alone which professes to have received a divine command to 'go and teach all nations'; and it is only Christianity which acts upon such an injunction.

"Isolate, for a moment, the case of Regent's Town, and let it be regarded with close attention. Here is a single man but just escaped from a London workshop, employed in organizing, civilizing, and humanizing a large body of rescued slaves, of

* "The Eclipse of Faith," p. 218.

a different race and of various other tongues. In a wonderfully short space of time he so gains the affections of these poor savages that a large Christian village arises almost as if by magic. Streets and gardens, a church and schools, fields and farmyards, are occupied and cultivated by hundreds of willing hearts and hands. *At once*, without any delay, a congregation of redeemed and saved men and women is seen. The church is filled to overflowing; the schools are crowded with eager learners; hundreds press forward to beg for the benefit of the Christian sacraments; meanwhile, industry and its fruits abound on every side, and purity of morals such as no English village knows universally prevails. Such are the results of even three or four years' labor; may we not reasonably ask, When did the religion of Rome or of the East, or when did the philanthropy of rationalistic philosophers, produce such a wondrous transformation as this?

"It is well that men should thoroughly understand that Christianity is *alone* in the world as a religion. There is no other faith which even pretends to be made for mankind; and there is no other the adherents to which make any attempt to diffuse it among mankind. The reason is easily discernible. The various forms of heathenism have all one original and one patron: they constitute different provinces of the one kingdom of 'the god of this world.' They do not make war upon each other, for 'if Satan be divided against Satan, how shall his kingdom stand?' But with the religion of Christ the case is wholly different. Five hundred years before it was distinctly manifested, a prophet was inspired to foretell that after the Assyrian, Persian, Macedonian, and Roman empires a totally different power should arise—'a stone, cut out without hands, which should become a great mountain, and should fill the whole earth.' And Christ Himself, when departing from the earth for a season, said to His disciples, 'All power is given unto Me in heaven and in earth. Go ye therefore, and teach all nations.'

"This command was given eighteen hundred years ago, in the land of Palestine, and it was addressed to a few poor fishermen and artisans. And in this nineteenth century, lamentably as the injunction has been neglected, we still see several hundreds of men traversing, like Johnson and Williams, different regions of the earth, braving the pestilence here and the club of the savage there, and even rejoicing to lay down their lives in such a cause.

"The prediction, the command, and the fact which are at this moment before our eyes, should all be taken in connection; and if this be done, the sincere seeker after truth will find that which admits of but one reasonable solution.

"But let us for a moment take a still larger view, and compare the narrative we have just closed with the works and ways of men in general, taking for the stronger argument men in their most civilized and humanized condition.

"What are the thoughts and pursuits of men in society, even if we look chiefly to the most refined and humanized of the species—nay, even to men associated together in Christian churches? Are they not bent, for the most part, either on the acquisition of money, or on the pursuit of what is called pleasure? Taking even the more respectable and moral classes apart from the rest, do we not find that either the pursuit of wealth, or the enjoyment of the things procured by wealth, is the one predominant idea?

"What a contrast is furnished by the memoir we

are closing! A most active and energetic mind,
engaged for seven years in one engrossing pursuit,
and that pursuit so far above the sordid aims of
men in general, that his letters, journals, and re-
ports for a long series of years may be searched,
and not a thought connected with self, selfish gains,
or selfish enjoyments will be found. As, in paradise of old, and in the paradise yet to be revealed,
all thoughts of such things would seem absurd, re-
volting, and out of place, so, in the higher atmosphere to which Johnson had attained, he seems to
have left such thoughts behind. He had his 'food
and raiment' provided for him, and he had his work
to do; that done, there only remained the blessed
termination: 'God calls me, and this night I shall
be with Him.'

"It is true that some few cases of less selfish and
sordid views and feelings do now and then occur in
the world at large. One higher and nobler aspect
of human labors and human ambition has been
presented in the most emphatic way while these
closing pages were passing through the press. All
that human nature in its noblest and best condition
could offer has just passed before us, in the person
of the greatest warrior of Europe, now on his way
to his last earthly resting-place.* Let us honor, as
David honored Abner, the memory of one of the
powerful of the earth, who acknowledged heaven's
law, *subjection*, and knew it to be his safest and
wisest course to follow only the dictates of *duty*.
But while we rejoice in such an example, let us
rightly appreciate the sphere and character of his
labors. The noblest of his kind, still that kind was
not the highest. The warrior has to do with earth
only; the preacher of the gospel has to do with

* The reference is to the Duke of Wellington, who died
September 14, 1852, and was buried in Westminster Abbey.

heaven. So long as our present condition lasts, which will be but a few years longer, Waterloo will be one of earth's most thrilling names. It decided the fate of empires; it gave Europe 'rest for forty years.' But when the transitory things of the present world shall have vanished, and the *real* and *eternal* shall rise in their proper form and consistency, then Waterloo and Agincourt and Marathon will be remembered only with wonder and with pity, while such names as Bethelsdorp, Raiatoia, and Regent's Town will be 'had in everlasting remembrance.'

"What is the brightest hope held out in God's Word to the truest and most faithful of His servants? We know, indeed, that salvation is the common hope of all; that to be admitted 'within the gates of the city' is the humble trust of every believer. But our Lord has said, 'In My Father's house are many mansions.' His apostle adds that 'one star differeth from another star in glory.' The meaning of the gospel parable is not dubious, which relates that the king rewarded his servants with authority over two cities, over five, or over ten, according to their previous success in his service. Now the most glorious promise of future bliss that is to be found in Holy Scripture is that which declares that 'they that be wise shall shine as the brightness of the firmament; and *they that turn many to righteousness, as the stars for ever and ever.*'

"Behold, then, a poor mechanic, laboring in Whitechapel, 'almost naked and in want of food.' God suddenly, without any human aid, 'speaks to his heart.'* At once does he respond to the call; at once does he spring 'out of darkness into marvelous light.' Soon after, he hears of the wretched state of the heathen, and he steps forward with

* Hos. ii. 14, margin.

'Here am I; send me.' He is sent, and for seven years each month's labor is a visible inroad on the kingdom of Satan. All that he does, whether in teaching or exhorting or withstanding error, is done with the whole heart. His success is almost without a precedent. Doubtless a whole company of redeemed souls went before him to paradise. The church built up by him in six short years, although long afflicted and left destitute, endured, and is a living and thriving church at this day. Its candlestick remains, a light to all western Africa. And what of its founder? Gone, to shine 'as the stars for ever and ever'! Few, when seated in 'heavenly places,' far above myriads of the learned, the wealthy, the honored, and the powerful of the Christian church—few, very few, will cry louder than he, 'O the depth of the riches both of the wisdom and knowledge of God! how unsearchable are His judgments, and His ways past finding out!'"

www.ingramcontent.com/pod-product-compliance
Lightning Source LLC
Chambersburg PA
CBHW031728230426
43669CB00007B/280